Differentiating for Inclus

Target Ladders:

Speech, Language and Communication Needs

Susan Lyon

with

Neil Barrett Sarah Boulter Anna Heydon
Jo Westwood Jennifer Williams

Series editor Kate Ruttle

LDA has a range of learning development aids to help children with special needs and general learning difficulties. For our full range and helpful information, visit www.ldalearning.com.

The products mentioned in this book are available from LDA, though not all have been created or published by LDA.

Acknowledgements

The authors would like to thank the management of the Paediatric Speech and Language Therapy Service, East Coast Community Healthcare CIC, for their support.

Permission to photocopy

Target Ladders: Speech, Language and Communication Needs

ISBN 978-1-85503-550-8

© 2013 Susan Lyon/East Coast Community Healthcare CIC

First published 2013
Reprinted 2014
Printed in the UK for LDA

LDA, Findel Education, Hyde Buildings, Ashton Road, Hyde, Cheshire, SK14 4SH

Contents

Closing the gap

Although schools are trying to reduce the number of children on their Special Educational Need (SEN) registers, the array of learning difficulties faced by the children is not changing or diminishing. In many areas, the responsibility for identifying learning difficulties, and supporting the children, is being thrust more onto schools because the external services hitherto available to support identification and remediation are fast disappearing. In most primary schools, the responsibility for tackling children's learning challenges continues to lie with class teachers and Special Educational Needs Coordinators (SENCos), many of whom are non-specialists.

Following the Bew Report of 2011, the focus for OFSTED inspections is changing from a scrutiny of the attainment of the middle and high achievers to that of the progress made by the children with the lowest attainment. Inspectors are now looking for evidence that schools are working to 'close the gap'. The first step in closing the gap is to identify what learners can already do.

Case study

Chloe (6 years) lacked confidence in social situations and showed delayed play and interaction skills, though these skills seemed to be following a fairly typical pattern of development. Her targets focused on her social play and social interaction, so her teacher introduced opportunities for focused play sessions during playtimes in order to build her capacity for co-operative play, as well as daily opportunities to play turn-taking games. This intervention enabled Chloe to access a curriculum that developed her play and interaction skills without impacting significantly on her social and curriculum time in the classroom.

Whether individual targets are recorded on an Individual Education Plan (IEP), an internal target sheet, a Record of Progress or some other mechanism, the fact remains that these children continue to need small steps targets in order to clarify learning priorities and give the children a sense of achievement when they tick off another target.

The *Target Ladders* titles focus on one SEN at a time, in order that the range of difficulties and challenges facing young people with that SEN can be acknowledged. If any child in your care has any of the behaviours or difficulties addressed by a book in this series, then the targets listed in that book should be helpful and appropriate.

The *Target Ladders* books aim to support you in the following ways:

- Focusing on what a child *can* do, rather than what they cannot do, in order to identify next steps.
- Presenting 'small steps' targets for children.
- Suggesting strategies and activities you may find helpful in order to achieve the targets.
- Giving you the information you need to use your professional judgement and understanding of the child in determining priorities for learning.
- Recognising that every child is different and will follow their own pathway through the targets.
- Giving you an overview of the range of difficulties experienced by children with a particular SEN. Not all children will experience all of the difficulties, but once you know and understand the implications of the SEN, it gives you a better understanding as to a child's learning priorities.
- Providing a system for setting and monitoring targets which can replace or complement IEPs.

Setting useful targets for a child can be tricky. But '*I don't understand what she says*' is not a constructive statement when deciding what the next steps should be. In order to support the child, you need to find out first what they *can* do already and then break down the next steps. You are then in a good position to set targets and consider interventions.

Case study

Katie was in Year 5. She was referred to the school SENCo by her teacher because Katie consistently seemed to 'miss the point' in lessons, she was very disorganised and she often copied other children. No particular difficulties had been identified by previous teachers. Further discussion between the SENCo, Katie's teacher and her parents revealed the fact that Katie increasingly needed a lot of visual support to follow instructions both at home and at school and she was struggling to maintain friendships. School-based tests established that Katie's comprehension of spoken language was at around age 5 to 6. The gap between Katie's comprehension age and her chronological age would account both for her difficulty in gathering information and also her social difficulties: by the time most children are aged between 9 and 10, the language which dominates their social experiences is fast-moving and a child who cannot keep up will be increasingly isolated.

Using the *Target Ladders* books will enable both non-specialist teachers and SENCos to identify appropriate learning goals for independent learning, to adapt the suggested strategies or ideas for their own pupils, and to begin to impact on children's Speech, Language and Communication Needs in order to close the gap between these children and their peers.

How to use this book

You will find a simple five-step summary of how to use this book on page 9.

Every child with Speech, Language and Communication Needs (SLCN) has different strengths and weaknesses. The priority for addressing these will be determined by the difficulties currently being faced by the child and will depend on your professional judgement, supported by the child's current anxieties.

To support you with focused target setting, the book is structured as follows:

- Seven different Aspects of SLCN have been identified (see Fig. 1 opposite). Think about the child's difficulties: which of these Aspects is causing most concern at the moment?
- Within each Aspect there are three or four different Target Ladders, each based on a particular area of challenge. This is intended to help you to think carefully about precisely where the barrier may be.
- The relevant Target Ladder can then be used to identify the 'next step' target for the child.
- Suggested activities and strategies offer classroom-friendly ideas so you can support the child to meet their target.

For example, as you can see in the chart opposite, difficulties with Aspect 6: Social communication can be subdivided into specific areas to work on: Social understanding, Pragmatic understanding, Pragmatic use of language and Non-verbal pragmatics. Each Target Ladder contains up to 32 targets.

Aspects, Target Ladders and Targets

Aspects

The seven different Aspects identified in this book describe contexts and difficulties which are frequently faced by children who have SLCN. In order to identify the most appropriate Aspect for a particular child, you will need to consider the most significant barrier for the child: for example, is it that they do not understand other people (comprehension), or that other people do not understand them (speech)?

The Aspects of SLCN identified in this book are:

1 Early communication
2 Attention control
3 Play and social interaction
4 Comprehension
5 Expressive language
6 Social communication
7 Phonological awareness, auditory discrimination and speech.

Target Ladders

Each of the Aspects is further subdivided into three or four Target Ladders, each of which addresses different parts of the Aspect. These enable you to develop your understanding of the child's individual needs, 'drilling down' to assist you to identify the child's particular strengths and weaknesses. The Target Ladders are set out on pages 46–95.

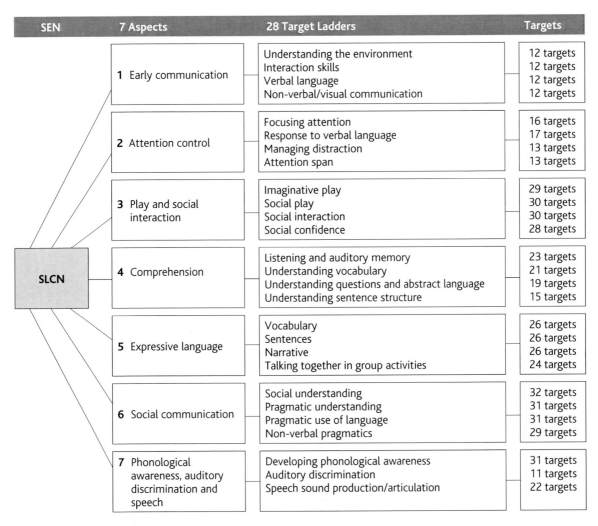

SEN	7 Aspects	28 Target Ladders	Targets
SLCN	1 Early communication	Understanding the environment Interaction skills Verbal language Non-verbal/visual communication	12 targets 12 targets 12 targets 12 targets
	2 Attention control	Focusing attention Response to verbal language Managing distraction Attention span	16 targets 17 targets 13 targets 13 targets
	3 Play and social interaction	Imaginative play Social play Social interaction Social confidence	29 targets 30 targets 30 targets 28 targets
	4 Comprehension	Listening and auditory memory Understanding vocabulary Understanding questions and abstract language Understanding sentence structure	23 targets 21 targets 19 targets 15 targets
	5 Expressive language	Vocabulary Sentences Narrative Talking together in group activities	26 targets 26 targets 26 targets 24 targets
	6 Social communication	Social understanding Pragmatic understanding Pragmatic use of language Non-verbal pragmatics	32 targets 31 targets 31 targets 29 targets
	7 Phonological awareness, auditory discrimination and speech	Developing phonological awareness Auditory discrimination Speech sound production/articulation	31 targets 11 targets 22 targets

Fig. 1: The structure of *Target Ladders: SLCN*. Each Aspect of SLCN has three or four Target Ladders, each with up to 32 individual targets.

Targets

There are up to 32 targets in each Target Ladder, with the simplest labelled with the letter 'A', then moving through the alphabet up to 'M', which are the most difficult. In each Target Ladder there are up to five rows that are labelled with the same letter, because all of the targets in those rows are at a similar developmental level. It is unlikely that any child will need to have all of the targets in each letter band: use your knowledge of the child to identify what they already know and to prioritise what is important.

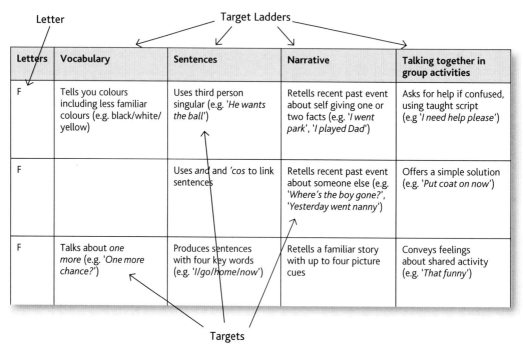

Fig. 2: Part of the Target Ladders table for Aspect 5: Expressive language (page 76), showing how targets are structured in the ladders.

Although within each Target Ladder rows with the same letter are similar, this is not the case between the different Target Ladders. So a child may have an A target in one ladder and a G target in another. Some of the Target Ladders start at a very early developmental level, whereas others assume a level of competence even in the A rows. Again, use your professional judgement and be guided by the child's abilities and needs. The letters are simply there to help you to identify targets which are at approximately the same developmental level within the same Target Ladder.

The targets are all written in positive language. This is to support you when you:

- look through them to find out what the child *can already* do;
- use them as the basis of the target you set for the child.

As you track the statements through each ladder, identifying what the child can already do, be aware of missed steps. If a child has missed one of the steps, further progress up that ladder may be insecure. Many children learn to mask the missed step, using developing skills in other areas to help them, but the time may come when the missed step will cause difficulties.

Activities and strategies to achieve the targets

In the Target Ladders on pages 46–95, targets are listed on left-hand pages. The corresponding right-hand pages offer ideas for activities and strategies that you might use to help to achieve the targets. These are suggestions only – but they have all been used successfully in classrooms and are accepted good practice. Here, however, the activities are shown at the point in the developmental process at which they are likely to make the most impact.

The suggested activities can often be adapted to work for a range of targets within this stage of the ladder. For this reason, activities are generally not linked to individual targets.

How to set targets: A five-step summary

1. **Use Fig. 1 on page 7 to identify the one or two Aspects of SLCN that are most challenging for the child.** Please use the list of indicators on pages 26–27 for guidance.

2. **Turn to the Scope and Sequence Charts on pages 11–18.** These charts will help you pinpoint the specific targets you need – a more detailed explanation is given on page 11. The Scope and Sequence charts show the *upper limit* of the targets reached in each Target Ladder in each Aspect. Use these to gain an indication of where in the book you are likely to find appropriate targets.

3. **In the Target Ladders tables on pages 46–95, locate the targets** that you have identified from the Scope and Sequence charts and pinpoint specific ones for the child to work towards.

4. **Photocopy or print out from the CD the relevant targets page** so that you can:
   - highlight and date those the child can already do;
   - identify the next priorities.

5. **Use the Record of Progress sheet on page 20** to create a copy of the targets for the child or their parents.

Making the most of Target Ladders

You may find the following tips helpful when setting your targets.

- If you are not sure which Aspect to highlight for a child:
  - think about your main concerns about that child's learning;
  - talk to the child about what they would like to improve;
  - discuss targets with the child's parents/carers.

A target that the child wants to improve is more likely to be successful.

- Once you have identified the Aspect, use the Scope and Sequence charts on pages 12–18 to identify the most beneficial Target Ladder and ascertain which page to start on.
    - Look for any 'missed steps', and target those first. The child is likely to find success fairly quickly and will be motivated to continue to try to reach new targets.
    - Talk to the child and agree an appropriate target based on your skills inventory. Again, targets which the child is aware of tend to be achieved most quickly and are motivational.
- The target does not have to be the lowest unachieved statement in any ladder: use your professional judgement and knowledge of the child to identify the most useful and important target for the child.
- No child will follow all of the targets in precisely the order listed. Use your professional judgement, and your knowledge about what the child can already do, to identify the most appropriate target and be realistic in your expectations. There may be some zigzagging up and down a column.
- When setting targets, always ask yourself practical questions:
    - What can I put in place in order to enable the child to meet the targets?
    - Which people and resources are available to support the child?
    - What is the likelihood of a child achieving a target within the next half-term?
    - Which targets have been agreed with other children in the class?

It is important that the targets you set are realistic considering the time, the adult support and the resources available.

Once you have identified what the child can already achieve, continue to highlight and update the sheets each time the child achieves a new target. Celebrate progress with the child – while, at the same time, constantly checking to ensure that previously achieved targets remain secure. If any target becomes insecure, revisit it briefly, without setting a formal target, in order to give the child an opportunity to consolidate the skill without feeling that they are going backwards in their achievements.

Scope and Sequence charts

The Scope and Sequence charts can be used to help you to pinpoint targets, following the advice on the preceding pages. Once you have identified the Aspect(s) you wish to focus on:

1. Find the relevant page in the Scope and Sequence charts on pages 12–18. Look for the Aspect name here:

2. Identify the Target Ladder(s) that matches the skills you wish to target. Look for the names of the ladders here:

3. Read down the list of targets here: The targets shown here are from the highest level for the ladder on that page. If the first target listed is too easy, look at the next target beneath it. Continue down the list until you reach a target that is beyond the child's current attainment.

4. Find the page number, shown here: Turn to that page and read all the targets on it. One of them should be appropriate. If not, turn to the previous or subsequent page.

Scope and Sequence Aspect 4: Comprehension

Listening and auditory memory

Page	Letters	Target Ladder focus	Focus of suggestions
64	A–C	Enjoys listening to a short story for 2–5 minutes	Listening games
66	D–E	Remembers a list of up to four different objects	Remember remember
68	F–I	Suggests solutions to simple problems or riddles presented orally	What am I?
70	J–M	Is able to use strategies to help remember instructions	Guided listening

Understanding vocabulary

Page	Letters	Target Ladder focus	Focus of suggestions
64	A–C	Sorts and selects objects by function	What does it do?
66	D–E	Understands more advanced positional words	Position words
68	F–I	Knows which objects belong in a category and which do not	Word families
70	J–L	Understands verbs used in curriculum	Pre-teaching

Fig. 3: Part of the Scope and Sequence chart for Aspect 4 (see page 15).

Bear in mind the following:

- The wording of the target may not be precisely accurate for your child. Modify it to make it appropriate.
- Different children may meet the target statements in a slightly different order. The order shown is approximate and true for many children. Adapt the order in which you set the targets for the individual child.
- No child is expected to have all of the targets on the page. A range of small-steps targets is shown in order to give you the widest possible variety of targets from which to select.
- If you cannot find a target which meets your needs, use the other targets to give you an idea of the level expected, and write your own target. It is important that all of the targets on the Record of Progress are appropriate for the individual child.

Scope and Sequence Aspect 1: Early communication

Understanding the environment

Page	Letters	Target Ladder focus	Focus of suggestions
46	A–C	Can be supported using objects of reference to follow a series of events during the day	Objects of reference
48	D–G	Independently accesses a visual timetable to work through a series of up to four events	Visual timetables

Interaction skills

Page	Letters	Target Ladder focus	Focus of suggestions
46	A–C	Enjoys simple 'people-games' and is becoming a more active participant	People-play
48	D–G	Initiates interaction with other children by making eye contact or handing over an object	Joint attention

Verbal language

Page	Letters	Target Ladder focus	Focus of suggestions
46	A–C	Understands simple instructions with an accompanying gesture	First words
48	D–G	Understands at least 50 words	

Non-verbal/visual communication

Page	Letters	Target Ladder focus	Focus of suggestions
46	A–C	Points to people or objects to request or show interest	Objects of reference People-play
48	D–G	Uses a wide range of signs or symbols to request and comment	Introducing signs and symbols

Scope and Sequence Aspect 2: Attention control

Focusing attention

Page	Letters	Target Ladder focus	Focus of suggestions
50	A–D	Follows visual or auditory prompt to pay attention	Getting the child's attention Visual prompts
52	E–G	Knows when it is their turn and re-engages attention	Taking turns
54	H–J	Is able to indicate willingness to get involved by putting hand up	Using photos as a behaviour prompt

Response to verbal language

Page	Letters	Target Ladder focus	Focus of suggestions
50	A–D	Alternates full attention (visual and auditory) between the speaker and the task without prompting	Switching focus of attention
52	E–G	Begins to understand main point of simple teacher talk	Listening and looking
54	H–J	Picks up more detailed information from teacher talk	Listening skills Picture Mind Maps

Managing distraction

Page	Letters	Target Ladder focus	Focus of suggestions
50	A–D	Is able to filter out distractions and keep engaged during small-group activities	
52	E–G	Listens and attends as part of a small group for short activities (e.g. 2 minutes each)	Sustaining attention in a small group Listening and looking
54	H–J	Filters out 'background' talk in class	Talking about attention

Attention span

Page	Letters	Target Ladder focus	Focus of suggestions
50	A–D	Listens to a short story from a picture book for up to 5 minutes in a group	Good listening
52	E–G	Maintains attention on chosen task for 5 minutes	Sustaining attention in a small group Sharing a focus of attention
54	H–J	Completes activity in busy classroom while socialising for 15 to 30 minutes	Wet playtime challenge

Scope and Sequence Aspect 3: Play and social interaction

Imaginative play

Page	Letters	Target Ladder focus	Focus of suggestions
56	A–B	Shows functional play skills	Stimulate the senses Hiding games
58	C–E	Uses one object to represent another	Learning to pretend
60	F–G	Plays purposefully and imaginatively with small world toys for extended periods	Supporting imaginative play
62	H–L	Increasingly distinguishes between fact and fantasy during imaginative play	Fact and fantasy

Social play

Page	Letters	Target Ladder focus	Focus of suggestions
56	A–B	Enjoys simple 'people games'	Joining in
58	C–E	Shares and takes turns in a short play activity with support	Guided play
60	F–G	Actively involves other children in play – listens to them and responds with talk	The rules of the game
62	H–M	Begins to show strategy in games such as Ludo® and Draughts	Team games

Social interaction

Page	Letters	Target Ladder focus	Focus of suggestions
56	A–B	Repeats actions/sounds if adult laughs at them	Joining in
58	C–E	Shows some early interaction with other children	Responding to communication
60	F–G	Is able to share, take turns and play by agreed rules	The rules of the game Modelling behaviours
62	H–M	Co-operates in group activities without direct adult guidance	Awareness of self and others

Social confidence

Page	Letters	Target Ladder focus	Focus of suggestions
56	A–B	Regularly initiates exchanges with familiar adult	Joining in Hiding games
58	C–E	Shows some interaction with other children, with support	Guided play
60	F–G	Asserts self appropriately with adults and other children	Social Stories™ Modelling behaviours
62	H–M	Has confidence to express opinion on ideas discussed	Ensure success

Scope and Sequence Aspect 4: Comprehension

Listening and auditory memory

Page	Letters	Target Ladder focus	Focus of suggestions
64	A–C	Enjoys listening to a short story for 2–5 minutes	Listening games
66	D–E	Remembers a list of up to four different objects	Remember remember
68	F–I	Suggests solutions to simple problems or riddles presented orally	What am I?
70	J–M	Is able to use strategies to help remember instructions	Guided listening

Understanding vocabulary

Page	Letters	Target Ladder focus	Focus of suggestions
64	A–C	Sorts and selects objects by function	What does it do?
66	D–E	Understands more advanced positional words	Position words
68	F–I	Knows which objects belong in a category and which do not	Word families
70	J–L	Understands verbs used in curriculum	Pre-teaching

Understanding questions and abstract language

Page	Letters	Target Ladder focus	Focus of suggestions
64	B–C	Identifies the correct object from a choice	Q and A
66	D–E	Can indicate what might happen next when carrying out a familiar routine such as cooking or getting dressed	What next?
68	F–H	Can understand questions requiring problem-solving from another person's point of view	Solve it
70	J–M	Understands idioms	Idioms

Understanding sentence structure

Page	Letters	Target Ladder focus	Focus of suggestions
64	A–C	Follows two-key-word instructions with familiar vocabulary	What does it do? Q and A
66	D–E	Understands regular plurals such as *cars*, *sweets* and *shoes*	More than one
68	F–H	Understands the use of negatives	Can't, won't, hasn't
70	M	Understands irregular plurals and irregular past tense	Playing with tenses

Scope and Sequence Aspect 5: Expressive language

Vocabulary

Page	Letters	Target Ladder focus	Focus of suggestions
72	A–C	Comments on size, texture or quantity	Naming Using abstract words
74	D–E	Tells you to place an object *behind/in front of/next to* something	Puppet play
76	F–H	Names items from one category	Sorting and grouping
78	I–L	Suggests synonyms for common words	Visual support

Sentences

Page	Letters	Target Ladder focus	Focus of suggestions
72	A–C	Uses four- to five-word phrases	Modelling and expanding
74	D–E	Uses pronouns *he*, *she*, *it*, *they* accurately with correct verb	Beginning pronouns Writing frame
76	F–H	Uses *can't/won't*	Hard to hear
78	I–L	Connects sentences with *however* and *actually*	Tenses Barrier games

Narrative

Page	Letters	Target Ladder focus	Focus of suggestions
72	A–C	Comments on what is happening during repetitive play sequences	Sequencing language
74	D–E	Tells you the next step in a familiar routine	What/where/who/when/why Puppet play
76	F–H	Describes an object/person/animal in a familiar story	Describing words
78	I–L	Creates an original story	Telling a story

Talking together in group activities

Page	Letters	Target Ladder focus	Focus of suggestions
72	A–C	Comments on what others are doing	Sequencing language
74	D–E	Asks *why*, *when* and *how* questions	What/where/who/when/why
76	F–H	Extends an idea	Using photos or pictures
78	I–L	Adapts what is said to the needs of the listener	Talking games

Scope and Sequence Aspect 6: Social communication

Social understanding			
Page	Letters	Target Ladder focus	Focus of suggestions
80	A–C	Accepts simple rules	Circle time activities
82	D–E	Conforms to classroom routines and rules	Catch them being good
84	F–H	Shows some social resilience	Problem-solving and negotiation
86	I–K	Is able to see other people's points of view	Managing difficult situations

Pragmatic understanding			
Page	Letters	Target Ladder focus	Focus of suggestions
80	A–C	Shows understanding of simple stories	Puppets and props
82	D–E	Recognises if others have not understood; responds appropriately to questions or requests for more information	Barrier games
84	F–H	Is aware of some metaphoric usages of language	Playing with language
86	I–K	Adapts style of speech to match the listener and the context	Exploring language use

Pragmatic use of language			
Page	Letters	Target Ladder focus	Focus of suggestions
80	A–C	Is able to create a very simple narrative	Puppets and props
82	D–E	Talks about feelings of characters in stories	Responding to stories
84	F–H	Is able to use language to bargain and negotiate	Problem-solving and negotiation
86	I–K	Uses cohesive devices in spoken language	Developing cohesion

Non-verbal pragmatics			
Page	Letters	Target Ladder focus	Focus of suggestions
80	A–C	Expresses feelings by gestures (as well as words)	Eye contact Vary your voice
82	D–E	Begins to control volume when speaking in class	Volume control
84	F–H	Is able to distinguish between contradictory words and tone of voice	Games to explore tone of voice
86	I–K	Recognises sarcasm and irony and responds appropriately	Sarcasm

Scope and Sequence Aspect 7: Phonological awareness, auditory discrimination and speech

Developing phonological awareness – with support			
Page	**Letters**	**Target Ladder focus**	**Focus of suggestions**
88	A–D	Claps out the number of syllables in one-, two- and three-syllable words in unison with teacher	Syllable Snap Spot the rhythm Find it Name that rhythm
90	E–F	Uses 'phonic fingers' to represent the number of sounds in a CVC word	Introducing analogy Using ICT Worksheets

Developing phonological awareness – independently			
Page	**Letters**	**Target Ladder focus**	**Focus of suggestions**
88	A–D	Claps out the number of syllables in one-, two- and three-syllable words independently	Syllable Snap Spot the rhythm Syllable sort
90	E–F	Segments phonetically simple words into individual sounds	Rhyming games Introducing analogy Worksheets

Auditory discrimination			
Page	**Letters**	**Target Ladder focus**	**Focus of suggestions**
92	G–J	Hears the difference between two speech sounds in CVC real words	Minimal pairs
94	K–L	Hears the difference between two phonemically related speech sounds in CVC real words	

Speech sound production/articulation			
Page	**Letters**	**Target Ladder focus**	**Focus of suggestions**
92	I–J	Imitates the target sound in a CVC word	Imitating and producing speech sounds
94	K–L	Uses the target sound in connected speech	Speech sound production

Using Target Ladders

Records of Progress

Creating a Record of Progress

If the child can communicate confidently, arrange to meet with them and ask them first to tell you what they are good at. Use pictures or symbols if necessary. Record their responses on the Record of Progress (RoP). A blank form is supplied for you to copy on page 20 and on the CD. Ask them then to tell you which areas they would most like to improve. If it is appropriate, choose something that addresses at least one of their issues as a target, so that the child feels some ownership of their RoP. If your school operates a Pupil Passport system, then you may want to amend the RoP form, but you will nonetheless need a sheet that can be annotated and amended.

As you add one or two more targets, talk to the child to check that they agree that each target is relevant and that they understand what they will need to do to achieve their targets. Targets that children don't know or care about are much harder for them to achieve. Limit the number of targets to a maximum of three. Remember, you do not need to use the precise wording of the targets given in this book: adapt the words to match the maturity and understanding of the learner.

If you are planning to use a published SLCN intervention, check to see what the recommended length of time for the intervention is. Monitor the impact of the intervention (see page 21) and review at regular intervals – at least half-termly – to see if there is an impact. If not, consider whether a different intervention would be more effective.

Principles for the effective use of a RoP include the following:

- The form must be 'live'. The child will need to have access to it at all times, as will all adults who work with the child, in order that it can be referred to, amended and updated regularly. It would be good practice to send a copy home for the parents/carers. If you think that the child is likely to lose or destroy their RoP, make a photocopy so that you can supply another.
- Together with the child, you have identified their priority areas to focus on. Management and support for these should be consistent across the school day and from all adults.
- As soon as each target has been achieved, according to the success criteria you agreed, the form should be dated and a 'next step' considered.
- When you set up the RoP, select a review date which is ideally about half a term ahead and no more than one term ahead. Don't wait until this date to identify that targets have been achieved, but on this date review progress towards all targets – or identified next steps – and agree new targets.
- If a target has not been achieved, consider why not. If possible, try a different approach to meeting the target. Having the same target over and over is likely to bore the child and put them off following their RoP.

RECORD OF PROGRESS

Name _____ Class _____ Date agreed _____ Review date _____

I am good at	My targets are	I will know that I have achieved my target when I can	Date when I achieved my target	Next steps
I would like to be better at				
It helps me when				

RoP number: _____ Targets approved by: Pupil _____ Teacher _____

SENCo _____ Parent/Carer _____ TA _____

Using Target Ladders

Monitoring a Record of Progress

In order to ensure that your Record of Progress (RoP) is used effectively, you need to monitor progress towards the targets each time you offer support. Use a monitoring sheet; a photocopiable example is given on page 22 and on the CD.

- Use a separate sheet – copied on to a different colour of paper – for each target.
- Write the child's name at the top of the sheet and the target underneath.
- On each occasion when someone works with the child towards the target, they should write the smaller, more specific target that you are working towards *during this session* in the box.
- They should then write a comment. On each occasion the child achieves the target during the session and then back in class, tick the box.

Comments should, as far as possible, refer to the child's behaviour and attitude rather than to their learning, which should be celebrated during the session. The intention is that these sheets should be used to create a cumulative record of a child's progress towards their target. The evidence here can be used to assess the impact of an intervention in order that its appropriateness can be evaluated swiftly and any additional actions can be taken promptly.

What precisely you record will depend on the type of support being offered and the nature of the target.

- If you are delivering a planned intervention, make a record of the unit/page/activity and a comment about the learning the child demonstrated. For example, a comment relating to a target about the child's ability to talk about past events might read: *Told me what we did in class this morning. Some accurate use of –ed ☺ (inaccurate: goed, maked).*
- If you are offering support in the classroom, you might want to comment on the child's learning over a few lessons. Focus on what the child has achieved in the lessons and whether the learning is secure.
- As a general principle, aim to include more positive than negative comments, and always try to balance a negative with a positive comment.

At the half-termly review of the RoP, collect together all of the monitoring sheets and look at the frequency of the comments against each target as well as the learning they reflect. If a child has had absences, or an intervention has not happened as often as planned, consider what impact that has had on the effectiveness of the intervention. If the intervention has gone as planned, look at the progress charted and ask yourself these questions:

- Is it swift enough? Is the intervention helping this child to close the gap? Is the adult working with the child the best person for the job?
- Is this the best intervention? Is there anything else you can reasonably do in school?
- What should happen next? If the intervention was successful, do you continue it, develop it, consolidate it or change to a different target?

At the end of the process, create a new RoP with the child and use a new monitoring sheet.

Monitoring the progress of _____ towards meeting

Target _____

Date	Target	Comment	Achieved			

Using Target Ladders

What are SLCN?

Speech, Language and Communication Needs (SLCN) is an umbrella term covering a range of difficulties that can affect a child's ability to access the school curriculum and make appropriate social relationships. I CAN, the children's communication charity (www.ican.org.uk), recognises that a child with SLCN:

- may have speech that is difficult to understand;
- may struggle to say words or sentences;
- may not understand words that are being used, or the instructions they hear;
- may have difficulties knowing how to talk and listen to others in a conversation.

Children may have just some or all of these difficulties; children are all very different.

I CAN claims that over one million children in the UK – that is, two or three in every primary classroom – have some kind of SLCN that requires specialist intervention.

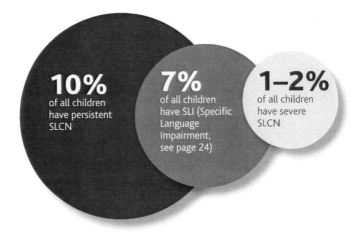

Fig. 4: Percentages of children with SLCN. From *I CAN Talk*, issue 9, 'Children with severe SLCN', online at http://www.ican.org.uk/~/media/Ican2/Whats%20the%20Issue/Evidence/ICAN_TalkSeries9.ashx.

Language is fundamental to every activity in the classroom – learning, thinking, communicating and making friends. For those children whose language is delayed, the school day can be confusing and stressful, and they can be excluded from many daily activities. They are not 'lazy' or 'stubborn'. Sometimes SLCNs are associated with other conditions – for example, cerebral palsy, cleft palate, hearing loss or Autistic Spectrum characteristics. Some children may have SLCN as part of a global developmental delay or due to environmental and emotional difficulties.

Other children have SLCN in the absence of any known neurological, intellectual, sensory or emotional difficulties. These children may be developing in line with their peers in all other areas and so their difficulties are specific to speech, language and communication. Such children may be referred to as having a **Specific Language Impairment (SLI)** or a Language Disorder.

Children with SLI have exceptional difficulty learning and generalising speech, language and communication skills. Their communication skills do not develop in the same way as other children's. There is no known cause for it. The speech and language difficulties in SLI are specific and persistent and are not due to an overall learning difficulty, hearing loss, environmental deprivation or Autistic Spectrum characteristics.

As children grow older, the role that language plays in their social and intellectual understanding increases as learning moves from the concrete to the abstract. So, comprehension at a level which is appropriate and adequate for a 6-year-old is inadequate for the learning and social needs of a 10-year-old. Although many of the targets in this book address early goals in the development of language, the targets are nonetheless relevant for older children whose language development is delayed or disordered.

Children aged 8+ who have receptive or expressive language difficulties are often 'hidden' in class. But if their receptive or expressive language is much below their chronological age (that is, working within the levels described in the book) the children will not make progress without some support – and support from a knowledgeable class teacher all day every day, using targets from this book, will encourage their language development.

The Royal College of Speech and Language Therapists (see their website at www.rcslt.org) tells us the following:

- Speech, Language and Communication Needs are the most common disability presenting in early childhood.
- In socially deprived areas there can be more than 17 children in each class with language skills below the average for their age. That is approximately 55 per cent. They may not require specialist help, but will need additional support to help them be included in class activities.
- The association between speech and language disorders and behavioural difficulties is well established.
- Communication difficulties impact upon children's social and emotional development as well as their ability to access the curriculum – particularly for literacy.
- Up to one-third of children with diagnosed communication problems will develop mental illness if untreated.

Identifying children with SLCN in your classroom

Often, speech, language and communication are thought of as a chain of skills, each dependent on the other. When we are communicating, we 'take in' information and then need to respond to it appropriately. These skills are often described as 'understanding/receptive language' (taking in the information) and 'expressive language' (responding to it).

The chances are very high that you have at least one, and probably two or more, children with SLCN in your classroom. Understanding the building blocks of communication will help you to adjust your practice to support these learners.

Consider the familiar question, asked most days in the classroom, '*Hands up if you're a packed lunch?*'

Children with **receptive language difficulties** may respond in any of the following ways:

- Abbie gives no response – she is still looking out the window because she has poor listening and attention skills.
- Claire runs over to the shelf and brings you her lunchbox because she understands only key words and simple sentences.
- David shouts '*No, I'm a boy. I'm not a packed lunch*', because he takes everything literally and may be on the Autistic Spectrum.
- Mina gives a monologue about what is in her lunchbox and what was in it yesterday because she has not learned to pick up cues about speaking appropriately.

During circle time you may recognise the following responses to the question, '*What did you do at the weekend?*' which may indicate **expressive language difficulties**:

- Erin is looking at you, appearing interested, but gives no response because she is still trying to decide what to say and organise her ideas.
- Fred gives a one- or two-word response, for example, '*shops ... play*' because he cannot remember the words he needs to tell you about swimming.
- Joao gives a telegrammatic response, such as '*me go shop him not buy car red*', because he cannot put words into sentences.
- Harry gives an unintelligible response, '*do deedide*' because he cannot use a wide range of speech sounds but is desperate to tell you about the seaside.

SLCN indicators

The following list is not intended to be used as an assessment tool. Instead it is a list of possible indicators of SLCN in children who are in Reception year or above, as a reminder of the complexity of needs with which SLCN can often present. Most aspects of SLCN will have implications for a child's performance and attainment across the taught curriculum, and in addition, for behaviour.

Although this list is not intended to be used as a screening tool, if you teach a child for whom you would tick 'yes' (when compared to the majority of children of the same age) to some of the following statements, it would be wise to seek further advice from a trained Speech and Language Therapist (SLT), and, in the interim, to follow general good practice for working with children with SLCN. (Note: If the child only has difficulties in the area of phonological awareness, consult an educational advisor, not an SLT.)

SPEECH, LANGUAGE AND COMMUNICATION PRESENTATION	Yes/No
Attention control	
Remains engrossed in an activity when others speak to them	
Frequently needs reminders to stop and listen	
Does not always notice what is shown or said to them	
Does not always notice what is shown or said to the group	
Play and social interaction	
Finds it difficult to tolerate others playing closely alongside	
Finds it difficult to join in others' play	
Shows limited communication about their play	
Has restricted range of play interests	
Has shorter concentration span for play than for other learning activities	
Shows little pretend/imaginative play	
Social communication	
Appears to be 'in own little world'	
Uses echolalia (i.e. copies words, phrases or chunks of dialogue with no apparent understanding of them, either immediately or later on)	
Struggles with changes in routine or changes to expectations	
Shows limited understanding of what the listener may already know or need to know	
Shows lack of interest in the topics most of their peers talk about	
Seems to communicate relatively little with others, considering their language/intellectual ability	
Often wants to talk about topics that are unusual for their age group (e.g. volcanoes, folk music)	
Uses lots of deviations and shares inconsequential information, without communicating the main point	
Is socially isolated as a result of difficulties in communicating with peers	
Receptive language (understanding of spoken language)	
Is fidgety during longer teacher-talk sessions	
Shows poor concentration for verbal tasks, but concentrates well for practical tasks	
Sometimes does not answer questions with appropriate information	
Responds well to short, simple instructions, but struggles with longer ones	
Relies on copying peers after having been given verbal instructions	
Asks you to repeat things you have already said	
Relies on non-verbal cues (often following others, using visual clues or following routines)	
Finds it difficult to follow instructions	
Avoids contributing during whole-class sessions	
Confuses *wh-* words in questions and gives inappropriate answers	
Needs considerable take-up time to process what you have said or asked	

Expressive language	
Uses only short phrases/sentences	
Often omits 'little words' (grammatical words such as *the, is, and*)	
Uses limited vocabulary, and some words may do a lot of 'work' in talk (e.g. *do, thing, that*)	
Seems to rely on learned social phrases, or familiar conversation-fillers	
Often misses out suffixes and inflections from sentences (e.g. *ing, ed, -s*)	
Uses rather muddled sentences, with words in an odd order	
Ideas seem to be muddled, making the communication hard to understand	
Sometimes uses words incorrectly (e.g. *throwed* instead of *throw*)	
Has difficulties in 'finding' words and sometimes appears to have briefly forgotten them	
Often uses the wrong word, although the word used may be related to the target word (e.g. *fridge* instead of *dishwasher*)	
Finds it hard to be specific, even when they can communicate general ideas	
Speech clarity	
Speech is difficult to understand for unfamiliar people, or out of context	
Some sounds are consistently not pronounced in speech (Note: consonant clusters may not be present during the Reception year, and /r/ and /th/ sounds are typically not used before age 7 years)	
Misses out sounds or syllables in words or sentences	
Substitutes one sound for another in speech (e.g. says *hunny* instead of *sunny*)	
Phonological awareness	
Finds it hard to generate rhyming words	
Finds it hard to recognise whether two words rhyme	
Has difficulty hearing whether two sounds are the same or different	
Struggles to learn phonics, matching letters to sounds	
Finds it hard to orally segment words for spelling or reading (e.g. '*m-u-g*')	
Finds it difficult to identify the number of syllables in a word	
Speech fluency	
Has a stammer	
Sometimes gets stuck on a word (so that no sound comes out immediately)	
Face is sometimes tense when the child is trying to speak	
Motor tics (e.g. blinking) begin when trying to speak	
Speech is so fast that it appears jumbled together	
Confidence about speaking	
Never speaks at school/in front of a group, even though they speak in other situations (e.g. at home)	
Often seems anxious about speaking	
Voice	
Voice is often hoarse, in the absence of a cold/throat infection	
Voice is frequently too loud or too quiet	

Supporting early communication skills

The foundations of communication are laid long before a child is able to say their first word. The development of the skills which underpin communication are often depicted in the form of a pyramid.

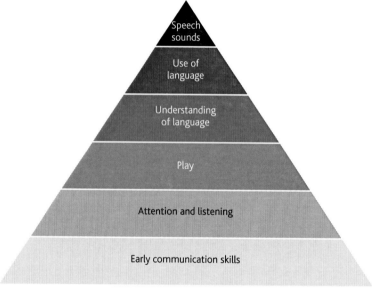

Fig. 5: The skills which underpin communication.

It is essential for the skills at the bottom of the pyramid to develop before we can expect the understanding and use of language to emerge. That is why this book contains sections around social interaction, attention and play as well as more specifically about language and communication – these skills are all closely interlinked and develop in conjunction with each other.

Signs, symbols and objects

Communication occurs, even without the use of spoken words. Increasingly, children with difficulties which include SLCN are integrated into mainstream schools, and these include children who are pre-lingual and who communicate through touch, gesture and look. It is important that all these forms of communication are valued and developed: a child will only learn what communication is about if their attempts at interaction are received and a response gained. Children who don't communicate effectively using spoken language are likely to need additional visual support – such as the use of objects, signs and symbols – to help them in their understanding and use of language in school.

- **Objects** may be useful to support communication if the child does not yet recognise pictures. 'Objects of reference' are objects which are linked to known events (for example, a bookbag may be used to indicate home time).
- **Signs** are an agreed system of using gestures and body movements to communicate.
- **Symbols** are simple pictures. They can be used either to show a child what is happening next (for example, on a timetable or Now and Next board), or for the child to communicate what they want (for example, using a choiceboard). These two uses of symbols should be kept separate so that the child does not become confused.

Signs, symbols and objects are useful to support communication for the following reasons:

- For many children, visual and tactile learning is easier than language learning.
- It is difficult to show children how to co-ordinate all the muscles and nerves needed to produce speech. But we may be able to help them use their hands to exchange a symbol or form a sign.
- Children often use gesture to communicate from an early age. Signing is an extension of this.
- Signs, symbols and objects more directly represent objects than spoken words, that is, they frequently *look like* the thing they are representing.
- A sign/symbol/object does not disappear as quickly as a spoken word does. This gives the child more thinking time.

The use of signs, symbols and objects is sometimes referred to as Augmentative and Alternative Communication (AAC). The most common forms of AAC used in schools include the following:

- A signing approach, such as Makaton, to support a child whose speech sounds are very disordered or whose oral language is only just beginning.
- Picture Exchange Communication System (PECS) with children on the Autistic Spectrum.
- An app such as Proloquo2go (available to purchase from http://www.assistiveware.com/product/proloquo2go) for children who are able to initiate communication using signs and symbols.

This is not an exhaustive list of AAC approaches. In Reception classes, informal AACs are often encouraged. For example, a child may hold up a 'toilet token' to indicate a request to go to the toilet. As children get older, these supportive approaches often diminish, but it is important to continue their use for children who rely on them, especially children on the Autistic Spectrum.

The development of attention control

Children attend to stimuli in different ways, and their pattern of attention control has a significant impact on their learning style and their learning potential. As a child's ability to control the focus of their attention develops, the child also develops an awareness of their environment and starts to have thoughts together with plans about ways to develop their thoughts and experiences in a goal-oriented manner.

A certain level of maturity of attention control is required before a child can develop higher-order skills, such as using language and interacting purposefully with other individuals.

The levels of development of attention control, as identified by Reynell et al. (1978) are given below:

Level 1
Distracted by external stimuli (e.g. someone walking by)
Attends fleetingly to stimuli
Focus of attention is 'captured' by stimuli (i.e. attention is involuntary)

Level 2
Concentrates on a concrete task of their own choosing (i.e. attention is voluntary)
Cuts self off from external stimuli when concentrating (i.e. does not respond to adult and may appear wilful)

Level 3
Attends more automatically to adults, but attention remains single-channelled (i.e. is unable to attend to competing auditory and visual stimuli from different sources)
Shifts full attention to the speaker and then back to the activity, with an adult's help

Level 4
Controls focus of attention with more ease and purpose, but attention remains single-channelled
Alternates their full attention (visual and auditory) between the speaker and the task
Refocuses attention spontaneously (without the adult needing to focus and refocus that attention)

Level 5
Concentrates on what adult is saying without stopping what they are doing (attention is two-channelled)
Understands verbal instructions related to the task without interrupting the activity to look at the speaker
Listens and attends as part of a group, although attention span remains short
Picks up information in a more selective manner
Focuses on a single aspect of a complex situation

Level 6
Establishes and sustains integrated attention (i.e. integrates auditory, visual and tactile channels)
Listens and attends well in class
Shuts out unwanted, irrelevant information and concentrates only on the essential aspects (developing skill)

(From J. Cooper, M. Moodley and J. Reynell 1978, *Helping Language Development: A Developmental Programme for Children with Early Language Handicaps*, Edward Arnold Publishers.)

The majority of children achieve Level 6 by the time they are around 5 to 7 years old, but some children need additional support within the level they are currently working at in order to be able to progress through the levels. These levels are used as the basis for the focus on attention control in *Development Matters* (DfE 2012).

The importance of play

Many play skills are vital prerequisites to later language and social skills development. For example, through play children develop:

- listening and attention control;
- observation skills;
- imitation skills;
- concept formation;
- symbolic understanding;
- social confidence and enjoyment;
- reasoning skills, including conjecture;
- experimentation;
- social understanding;
- emotional understanding.

Imaginative play

The term 'imaginative play' includes symbolic/pretend play. This kind of play develops as part of a general symbolic understanding, which underpins the child's ability to understand and use language 'symbols' (signs, spoken words and, later, written words). Symbolic play also helps children to develop negotiation, self-regulation and problem-solving skills, along with other cognitive and reasoning skills.

Social play

Social play relates closely to the level of a child's social understanding and social communication skills. Children develop through the following stages:

- *solitary play* – to begin with, in a social play situation, children play on their own, and seem relatively uninterested in/unaware of what other children around them are doing;
- *parallel play* – later, children move to play alongside others (for example, at a doll's house/around a sand tray), but do not yet interact with other children, although they may watch them, and begin to copy their actions;
- *co-operative play* – children respond to others, initiate interaction about toys/play activities and increasingly share items and co-operate in order that organised group play and, later, group games can develop.

Note: Be careful when observing a child's play not to assume too quickly that you have seen symbolic or true pretend play. Some children, particularly those on the Autistic Spectrum, can copy quite elaborate sequences of play. For example a child may act out an extended scene from a popular TV programme, using various props in what appears to be imaginary play. Look for clues such as how the child responds if you introduce a new prop/character, or if another child comes to join in the play.

Disordered development of play

Some children show a 'disordered' pattern of play development rather than a delayed one (that is, their play skills are not developing in a typical way, or they have a somewhat patchy profile of play skills). For instance, many 4-year-olds enjoy sitting in a cardboard box and pretending that it's a car, making a car out of Duplo®, or running around 'being' a car and making a Vrrrm noise. However, a 4-year-old child with a disordered development may show relatively well-developed construction play skills (such as being able to build a vehicle using Duplo), but relatively poor symbolic play skills (for instance, showing bafflement when observing peers playing in cardboard box cars).

Some children's play may seem rather rigid or repetitive (for instance, they may act out the same play routine again and again, and resist others' attempts to encourage them to modify this). Where the development of play skills appears to be disordered and unbalanced in this way, children will generally need to be seen by more specialist professionals for assessment, advice and therapy.

The development of understanding

Children will typically understand more words and sentences than they actually use. If you have ever started to learn a foreign language you will know that to begin with what you hear is an indistinguishable noise but then you gradually 'pick up' more familiar sounds that may be words. You may link the word that sounds like 'hola' to a situation – it is used when you meet someone, everyone says it and smiles and kisses. So it is with children – they will link the sounds of a drink being prepared with an adult saying 'Do you want a drink?', often accompanied with a gesture that looks like drinking or showing the cup or bottle of drink and so on.

Understanding language starts with understanding single concrete words such as *Mum* and *book*, which are things that you can see and touch. Eventually children learn more abstract words such as *big/little*, *hard/soft*, *yesterday/tomorrow*. We cannot see and touch these words and they change according to context. For example, a toy car may be comparatively 'big' but then we go outside and suddenly the toy car is not 'big' anymore. Understanding that these terms are context-dependent is part of developing an understanding of the meaning of the words.

Then children hear and begin to understand sentences and learn that word order and word endings are very important. For example, the active sentence 'The boy pushed the girl' has the same meaning as the passive sentence 'The girl was pushed by the boy' but the more straightforward, active word order is easier to understand. The word endings in 'I've finished my work' and 'I'll finish my work' make the difference between having an intention to do something and having done it.

In addition to understanding language, children very quickly pick up on visual cues in their surroundings. Be aware that children's expertise at using non-verbal cues may disguise a lack of understanding of verbal information: a child does not have to understand any language at all to cope in a typical classroom. Think about children who come from overseas with no English and yet manage very well from the day they set foot in your classroom. Often, a teacher will say that a child 'understands everything I say' but this may be because teachers use so much intonation, gesture and body language that children can understand enough not to stand out from the crowd. This is particularly true of children with Speech and Language Impairment (SLI), who are often bright and can survive well into the primary years before a teacher starts to question their comprehension.

SLCN can impact upon both academic development and behaviour. For example, speech sound difficulties may result in particular difficulties in phonics and literacy. Children with language difficulties may learn to say the words aloud, but may struggle with comprehension, and their written language will show similar traits to disordered spoken language. Children with language difficulties may also find it hard to learn and apply early mathematical concepts (*more, less, same, different, add, subtract*). Organisation may be affected because of lack of understanding or difficulty with sequencing, and children may have genuine problems in understanding tasks or remembering homework. In terms of their behaviour, SLCN may result in low self-esteem, withdrawal, avoidance, frustration, social difficulties, misunderstandings and anger. For some children (especially older ones) these behavioural or academic problems may be more immediately obvious than the underlying speech or language difficulty. For any child with behavioural or academic difficulties it is worth considering whether there is an underlying speech or language need.

Pragmatics and the social use of language

'Pragmatics' is a way of describing social use of language and focuses in particular on:

- how we use language for different functions (for example, greeting, information, instructing, filling in background information for a listener);
- how we change language according to context (for example, talking to a young child, playground language versus classroom language);
- the rules for conversations (for example, turn-taking, staying on topic, rephrasing if the listener does not understand, use of non-verbal cues such as proximity, eye contact, facial expressions).

Pragmatics concerns the functional use of language. Children have to learn the various rules that apply to the way language is used for social purposes. There can be many different functions of language – including requesting things, refusing things, greeting people and gaining attention. Just as with other aspects of language development there is a roughly typical pattern of development. For instance, requesting, commenting and refusing are early functions seen in infants. But promising, making jokes and using sarcasm are later functions that do not normally develop until after the age of 6 years.

Pragmatics encompasses both **receptive** and **expressive** aspects. For instance a child must understand (at least partly) what it means when someone else points to an object before they can develop the ability to point to objects in a meaningful way themselves (for example, to request the object, or draw the other person's attention to it). Because of this, in this book Pragmatic understanding, and Pragmatic use of language, are different Target Ladders in Aspect 6: Social communication (although they overlap considerably).

Expressive language

Most children start expressing themselves from birth – crying, gurgling. This oral language develops through babbling into words. Then these are joined first into phrases and next into sentences.

- First words are usually linked to familiar everyday activities. '*Mummy*', '*No*', '*Drink*', '*More*'.
- Often children will use a favourite word to link to other words so that they construct short phrases: '*Daddy gone*', '*Mummy coat*', '*More juice*'.
- As children develop the ability to construct longer, more complex sentences they will of course make mistakes. Many children will confuse pronouns ('*she run*', '*him book*'), or tenses ('*I runned fast*') or conjunctions ('*I first that why I run fast*'). This is a normal stage of development as children experiment with the rules of grammar.

In the Reception class, many children are still making errors with pronouns, tenses and conjunctions but by the time they are 12, most children can speak and write in accurate and complex sentences. Children whose expressive language is lagging behind in primary school need to be identified and supported through targeted interventions.

To be successfully remembered, words need to be stored in our memory according to meaning (semantic cues) and what they sound like (phonological cues). With known and unknown words, always talk to the children about what we do with it, what it looks like, what it sounds like, what category it belongs to, what parts it has, what are its attributes and what sound it begins with. If a child is struggling to name something, help them by giving them cues from this list.

Talking together in small groups around a focused activity is essential if children are to develop their skills as speakers and listeners. In small-group situations they are able to describe, explain, invent, give instructions and so on. If a child gives an instruction or makes a statement that confuses the other children, there is instant meaningful feedback from others in the group, which gives clues to the speaker that they have to clarify their language use.

Social communication

It could be argued that social communication is the most important aspect of this book. The reason that language developed in humans is so that they could successfully communicate their social, emotional and physical needs.

Communication can happen without speech and language (for example, using non-verbal means such as rolling of eyes), but language serves no useful purpose unless it is combined with communicative intent and skill.

In a typical child's development, social communication and interaction skills are already developing well before the understanding and use of language emerge. For instance, most infants initiate interaction, respond to an adult's smiles and point to request items before they learn any verbal labels. So communication is in place before words and sentences emerge. Further communication development over the next few years of a child's life happens in a similar way. There will be more advanced understanding and use of social communication that will underpin later, more complex language development.

Social understanding

Social understanding means the ability to make sense of social situations and this includes social awareness and social reasoning. For instance, a child may sit alongside other children on the carpet during their first assembly without being told to – they have understood this from the situation and what they see the others doing. An important aspect of social understanding is the development of empathy (the ability to understand that others may see/feel/think/know differently from them).

Non-verbal communication

Most speech, language and communication specialists consider the understanding and use of non-verbal language to be an integral part of pragmatics. Non-verbal aspects of communication include:

- eye contact and eye gaze;
- turn-taking;

- facial expressions;
- body language (including posture and gesture);
- communication distance (proximity);
- rate of speech (including fluency);
- intonation, rhythm and word stress (including tone of voice);
- volume and pitch.

Pragmatic difficulties

Many children with speech and language difficulties also have pragmatic difficulties. Sometimes difficulties in one aspect of language development can cause pragmatic difficulties (for example, a child with significant memory difficulties may find it hard to tell jokes, or a child with word-finding difficulties will struggle to give clear verbal instructions), but often pragmatic difficulties have a separate cause. For example, children with an Autistic Spectrum condition have pragmatic difficulties, which is why their use of language can appear so disordered.

Means, reasons and opportunities

The concept of 'means, reasons and opportunities' was outlined by Della Money and Sue Thurman in 1994, and explains in a helpful way why functional communication requires equal interaction between these three aspects.

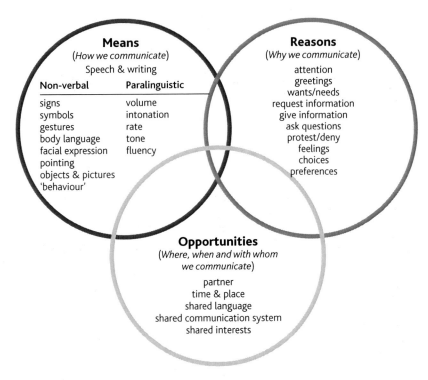

Fig. 6: Means, reasons and opportunities (from Della Money and Sue Thurman, 'Talkabout Communication', *College of Speech and Language Therapists Bulletin* 504, 1994, 12–13).

- Without the means of communication, you cannot express yourself.
- Without reasons for communication, there is no point in, nor need for, communication.
- Without the opportunities, there cannot be any communication.

It is useful to consider this model when considering the development of a child's social use of language.

Theory of mind

'Theory of mind' is the ability to show empathy and to understand that other people have knowledge/thoughts/desires that are different from one's own. Some children need to be taught these concepts. In *Teaching Children with Autism to Mind-Read: A Practical Guide* by Patricia Howlin, Simon Baron-Cohen and Julie Hadwin (1998) a structured approach to teaching the key concepts behind mental states in other people is suggested:

- *Photo facial recognition*: make feelings Lotto games by cutting out pictures from magazines (or buying commercial games). Sort the pictures and name the feelings.
- *Schematic facial recognition*: identify common features of faces showing each emotion (happy, sad, angry, afraid). Work together to create a simplistic face that can be used to indicate the emotion. For example, eyebrows slanting towards nose indicates anger; eyebrows slanting down towards ears indicates fear.
- *Situation-based emotions*: once children have learned to name some feelings, reflect back to them how they feel, using the emotion words. For example, '*I can see that you're feeling angry because X hit you.*' '*Well done. You got all your spellings right. You are probably feeling happy now.*'
- *Desire-based emotions*: use role-play and stories to talk about what characters want to happen.
- *Belief-based emotions*: start asking questions such as, '*What do you think [another child] is thinking about/wants to do?*' Initially, keep the contexts familiar and routine so the child has experienced the same situation and feeling themselves.

Speech and articulation

For many speech and language therapists, 'speech' – how we articulate the words we say – is the tip of the iceberg, as so many other complex skills need to be mastered first.

Speech sound development begins in early life. Consider babies of 6 months, who start vocalising and repeating syllable sequences with a limited range of (often unidentifiable) sounds. By 12 months these have become identifiable as vowel and consonant sounds and the child starts to use sounds to communicate their intentions.

Children produce their first recognisable and meaningful words between 1 and $1\frac{1}{2}$ years, but it will take several years for most children to make themselves understood. This is because consonant sounds (and sound sequences) can be difficult to make (articulation) and because children often make typical child-like 'sound replacements' or patterns (phonological processes). For example, when just starting to talk, children will typically simplify words. Try producing the /d/ /s/ and /sh/ sounds. They are all made with the tongue, but /d/ is easier to produce/articulate because your tongue needs to flick down from behind your top teeth. For /s/ and /sh/ your tongue needs to allow air to flow through a groove, so it requires greater control. As a result many children will typically substitute /d/ for the /s/ and /sh/ sounds when they first start using words. So *sea* and *Dee* will be produced identically and so will *deep* and *sheep*.

With time, children develop the ability to articulate the differences between speech sounds when talking – for example they learn to control their tongue so air can flow across it for /s/ and /sh/. Speech sounds, therefore, are acquired over several years and substitutions of sounds in words are part of normal speech sound development.

Typically children will make the speech sound *substitutions/replacements* shown in Table 1 when they are learning to talk.

Target sounds	Replaced by	Examples
Long /f/ /s/ /sh/	'Short' /b/ or /d/	fish → bish sea → dee shop → dop
Quiet (voiceless) /p/ /t/ /k/	Noisier (voiced) /b/ /d/ /g/	pea → bee tin → din cat → gat
Back of the mouth /k/ /g/	Front of the mouth /t/ /d/	car → tar gate → date
Clusters of sounds will be simplified		star → tar snake → nake

Table 1: Speech sound substitutions and replacements.

Speech sounds cannot be described independently of other aspects of language development. So it is important to consider the child's speech sound system within the context of their communication skills in general (such as attention, understanding of language, use of spoken language) in addition to environmental, physical, learning, developmental and psychological factors. Be aware that the most common reason that some children are not using particular sounds (or processes) is that they are not yet ready! Many children with *delayed* speech will develop normal speech spontaneously over time.

Other children have more specific speech sound difficulties, which do not always follow the usual pattern of speech sound development. Some of these children may not respond to the targets in this section and may need more direct and/or intensive support from a Speech and Language Therapist (SLT), particularly if they present with more disordered speech sound systems. If you have any doubts or concerns regarding a child's speech, please seek the advice of your local SLT.

It is not uncommon for the child with speech difficulties to have an intermittent hearing loss (such as 'glue ear') that could be affecting their ability to hear, listen to, discriminate and produce speech sounds. Has the child had a hearing test recently and what were the results? If there are *any* concerns regarding the child's hearing, these need to be addressed first.

How we make speech sounds

Some sounds in English are more similar than others. Understanding how sounds are made can help you to help the child to unpick any confusions. Sounds are articulated in different ways in the mouth, using the tongue and the lips.

Vowels

- Vowels are made with an open airstream. The air comes through the mouth and is shaped by the position of the tongue and lips.
- Use mirrors to look at the mouth making vowel sounds: ask children to say /ee/ and /oo/. What changes? Then try moving from /ar/ to /er/ and talk about what you see and what you feel your tongue doing.

Consonants

There are five basic categories of consonant sounds in English, the first three of which can be *voiced* – where the vocal cords vibrate (put your finger and thumb on either side of your voice box and say /zzzzz/ – feel the vibration), or *unvoiced* – where the vocal cords do not vibrate (say /ssss/ and note the voice box does not vibrate).

- *Plosives* are oral consonant sounds in which the airstream is momentarily blocked by the tongue or lips. Plosives can be voiced (for example, /b/ and /g/) or *unvoiced* (for example, /p/ and /k/).
- *Fricatives* are the longer 'hissing' sounds in which the airstream escapes through a nearly closed passage. Fricatives can be voiced or unvoiced (for example, /s/ and /v/).
- *Affricates* are made by a plosive being released into a fricative. Affricates can be voiced or unvoiced (for example, /ch/ and /dg/).
- *Nasals* are sounds in which the airstream is directed down the nose, rather than through the mouth. The sounds are varied by the position of the lips, teeth and tongue. All nasals are voiced (for example /m/).

- *Liquids and glides* are made when the tongue comes close to another part of the mouth without interrupting the flow of air. Liquids and glides are voiced (for example, /l/ and /r/).

Where in the mouth the sound is made	Between the lips (bilabial)	Lips and teeth (labio-dental)	Between the teeth (inter-dental)	Behind the teeth (alveolar)	Palate (alveo-palatal)	Back of the mouth (velar)	In the throat (glottal)
Plosive: unvoiced voiced	p b			t d		k g	Glottal stop
Fricative: unvoiced voiced		f v	th (*thin*) th (*this*)	s z	sh zh (*treasure*)		h
Affricate: unvoiced voiced					ch dg (*hedge*)		
Nasal	m			n		ng	
Glide/liquid	w			r l	y		

Table 2: Important relationships between the consonant sounds in English.

Understanding these relationships helps us to understand how easy it is to confuse certain sounds, particularly for children whose hearing is uncertain, owing to (for example) colds and glue ear. To a child who is relying to some extent on lip-reading /m/, /p/ and /b/ all look the same.

Teach children to explore the full range of sounds, using mirrors so that they can see how their mouth moves to shape the sounds they are making, and encouraging them to talk about how their tongue is touching the inside of their mouth.

Which sound to work on?

Children learn to use speech sounds in a developmental order that does not reflect the order that phonics are taught in school. Some sounds emerge in the first year of life through babbling, such as /baba/, /mama/, /dada/. Other sounds are not usually acquired until a child is older (for example, /l/ and /r/). Table 3 gives a summary of speech sound development.

Children learn these sounds first		These sounds tend to come when the child is around 3 to 5 years				These sounds come by age 7 or 8	
p	k	f	r	ch	dg	th (*thin*)	zh
m	g	v	l	sh	v	th (*this*)	
h	t		s	z			
n	d						
w	ng						
b							

Table 3: Speech sound development.

Within each group there is no particular order for the acquisition of the sound. Young children tend to use sounds they already know instead of sounds they are learning. For example, /b/ is used instead of /f/ (so *fall* becomes *ball*) and /d/ instead of /s/, /k/ and /g/ (so *sun* is pronounced *dun* and *gate* as *date*).

Children tend to learn sounds at the end of words first, then at the beginning and finally in the middle. They can say a sound individually before it is used in words and sounds are used in isolated words before they are used in running speech.

If the child is having difficulty copying a sound in isolation, try 'playing' with sounds in a less direct way, for example:

- using the tongue tip to touch the gum ridge behind the top teeth for sounds such as /n/ /t/ /d/ l/ /s/;
- smacking lips together to achieve lip sounds, such as /m/ /p/ /b/;
- opening the mouth wide to encourage back sounds, such as /c/k/ and /g/;
- gently biting the bottom lip with top teeth to achieve sounds /f/ and /v/.

If the child is struggling to achieve the target sound in isolation, do not progress through the hierarchy and seek the advice of an SLT.

An SLT may work on a range of sounds, or speech processes, but it is generally advisable for a non-specialist to work on only one sound at a time so as not to confuse the child.

When considering which sound to work on, ask yourself the following questions:

- Is the child using the sound elsewhere in a word?
- Can the child imitate the sound in isolation?
- Can they imitate the sound in a real word?
- Would you expect the child to be able to say this sound, given their age and developmental level?
- Does the child use all the sounds that you would expect at earlier levels?
- Can they hear the difference between the target sound versus another sound?
- Is there any physical/structural reason why they may not be able to make a specific sound? For example, front teeth missing may affect /f/; cleft lip/palate may affect production of many sounds.
- Is there a sound that they can make more easily that might be more beneficial to work on for progress and confidence?

If the answer to any of these questions is 'no', it is likely that the child is not yet developmentally ready to make the sound, so it is unlikely to be worth spending time focusing on it.

Developing phonological awareness

Phonological awareness skills are important for speech sound development and speech production. They are also implicated in children's growing proficiency in developing spoken language as well as in the acquisition of literacy skills. Major milestones are:

- Children as young as 3 years learn the pattern of speech and words with the help of songs and rhymes.
- By the age of approximately 4 years, children should be starting to play around with words and sounds and can usually be expected to 'Think of words that begin with the same sound ...'

- By the age of 5 years, most typically developing children will be able to think of rhyming words. Such phonological awareness skills are important for reading. Not surprisingly, some children with phonological problems may have associated reading difficulties.

When teaching phonological awareness, it is generally advisable to move from larger to smaller units of sound (that is, counting words, then syllables, before trying to count the number of sounds in a word). However, phonological awareness doesn't progress in a strictly linear sequence, so once children have, for example, understood the concept of syllables, they can progress to isolating sounds in words, but will need to revisit and refine their understanding of syllables at the same time. Concrete representations of sound (such as using counters or fingers to represent sounds, or blocks to represent syllables) may make it easier for children to manipulate the spoken form. Also, the use of pictures and objects may help to reduce the memory load.

Questions you may need to ask yourself include:

- Does the child understand what I am asking them to do?
- Do they understand concepts and vocabulary which we use when talking about sounds such as *same, different, beginning, end*?
- Are the activities within the child's ability to achieve?
- Is the child familiar with the letter-sound symbols that I'm using to teach phonics?
- Is the child's hearing satisfactory?

When introducing each activity, first model what is required yourself, so that the child knows what is expected of them.

Blending and segmenting

When helping children to hear the sounds in a word, teach the use of 'phonic fingers'. The child uses one index finger to point with and the fingers of the other hand to represent phonemes in a word. As the child says each new phoneme, they should point to a new phoneme finger (for example, *c-a-t* = three fingers). Once they have identified all of the phonemes, they should sweep their index finger across the phoneme fingers and say the whole word ('cat').

- Put a number of objects on a table. Use a puppet. Ask the child to give the puppet the *p-e-n* (and so on).
- Ask one child to hide one of your CVC objects while the others shut their eyes. Children can ask the hider questions, such as, 'What sound did the thing begin with?' 'What sound did it end with?'

There are a wide variety of commercially produced games and activity books, such as *CVC Word Spin* and *Fishing for Phonics*, to reinforce these vital stages of developing phonological awareness.

Creating an SLCN-friendly classroom

A communication-friendly classroom is a learner-friendly classroom, since all learners will benefit from strategies put in place to support those with SLCN. The following checklist is divided into sections centring on different kinds of difficulties experienced by children with SLCN. Different suggestions will be appropriate for different age groups and children. Some of the ideas will be appropriate for your situation, whereas there will be good reasons why others are less suitable for you. You should take from this list only what is relevant for the learners in your classroom and for you.

For children struggling to understand spoken language

If a child is struggling to understand what is said, you can help in the following ways:

- Sit the child near you during whole-class activities.
- Talk about whole-class rules for 'good listening' and have them prominently displayed with photographs of children demonstrating them.
- Make sure you say the child's name at the beginning of an instruction. They might not listen to *'Everyone sit down'* because *'Everyone'* is not their name.
- Think about their attention skills. Are they still at the 'rigid' stage of attention where they only do one activity at a time, ignoring everything else? If so, touch their arm, say their name, stop their activity and then give the instruction.
- Give your instructions in the order they are to be carried out. For example, *'Have you got a packed lunch? Then put up your hand.'*
- Limit your use of idioms, metaphors and sarcasm.
- Be aware of the demands you are making when giving an instruction. Be prepared to break it down into smaller steps.
  - Allow take-up time to give the child time to process what you asked and to organise their response.
  - Prepare the child to answer a question by warning them that you are going to ask one. For example, *'James, I'm going to ask Samir a question, then I'm going to ask you one'*.
- Use visual timetables, lists and pictures for as long as necessary to help children understand routines, prepare for change and organise themselves.

- Talk about what you are doing before, during and after. Use phrases such as *'First we ... and then we ... and last we ...'*. This helps organisation of thoughts, ideas and words.
- Use Mind Maps whenever you can, however young the child is. Mind Maps use categories and colour, and are permanent – all wonderful aids to a child confused by what they hear.
- Use non-verbal cues. Emphasise key words, nod or shake your head, and use clear facial expressions. Over 60 per cent of a message is understood in this way.

For children struggling to talk

If a child is struggling to communicate in speech, make sure you consider the following:
- Allow them to use a variety of means to get their message across – talking, signing, gesture, drawing, pointing to photos and symbols, and so on.
- Respond to what they say, rather than *how* they say it.
- Get on their level physically when talking.
- Do not correct mistakes of grammar, word order or pronunciation. Instead, repeat the sentence correctly so the child hears a good example of language. Repeating, emphasising and expanding are invaluable.
- Encourage the child to talk by making comments rather than asking questions. Instead of saying *'What are you playing with? What colour is it? Where did you find it?'*, try *'That's a big doll ... she's got red hair ... let's brush it'*.
- Use 'forced alternatives', such as, *'Is the boy eating an apple or drinking milk?'*
- Let the child listen to others first in a group activity so they can hear examples of appropriate answers.
- When you ask a question, allow time for the child to frame their answer. Try not to assume that they don't know because they have not replied instantly.
- Make use of subjects such as science and cooking in which you can verbalise, organise and sequence ideas.
- Make 'think, pair, share' a regular part of your classroom activities. When you ask a question which involves opinions:
  - first ask all children to think about their response;
  - then ask children to pair with a 'talk partner' to swap ideas and to firm up their opinions;
  - finally, invite children to share their ideas with a larger group.

  This approach gives all children the time to tell someone what they are thinking about, even if they cannot all tell the whole class, and gives children with SLCN the opportunity to frame their responses.
- Provide older children with SLCN with a credit-card type wallet containing written prompts including:
  - social prompts (such as, *'Can I please join your game?'*);
  - organisational prompts (such as, *'Please can you remind me what I have to do next?'*); and
  - curriculum prompts (such as, *'I'm sorry but I didn't understand what you said'*).

  Write each prompt on a separate credit-card sized slip of paper and allow the child to illustrate it.

- Use a home school book to give you an idea of what has been happening at home – this will help you tune into what a child is saying.
- Use activities designed to develop phonological awareness as often as possible with children whose speech is unclear.

Activities and strategies to promote communication in the classroom

Children who need additional support for communication benefit from games and activities which encourage talk. Most of these activities are referred to briefly in the Target Ladders, but are explained more fully here.

Now and Next boards

For children who are able to recognise pictures or photos, a Now and Next board can be used. Now and Next boards consist of just two pictures: the activity you are doing now, and the one that will happen next. They are the simplest form of visual timetable.

- Once an activity is finished, take the child to the Now and Next board, say 'Finished' and help the child to put the relevant picture into a 'Finished' box or envelope.
- Encourage the child to become independent in using the Now and Next board.

Visual timetables

Timetables can be arranged top to bottom (easier) or left to right (harder).

- Include key activities that structure the day, for example, registration → assembly → snack-time → playtime → free play → home time.
- Once the activity is finished, take the child to the timetable, say 'Finished' and help the child to put the picture into a 'Finished' box or envelope.

Encourage the child to become independent in going to their timetable when an activity is finished to post the symbol and find out what will happen next.

Barrier games

Encourage the use of descriptive vocabulary and sentences. One child 'speaks' and the other 'listens' so they will need a quiet area.

You will need:

- Two sets of identical equipment. For example, Lego bricks, paper and coloured pens, identical pictures to be coloured, farm animals and farm base (can be drawn on card).
- A barrier. This can be a big book or folder open and balanced upright between the two children.

The 'speaker' then gives the 'listener' instructions. For example, 'Colour the door on the house blue' or 'Put the cow in the field'. The listener and the speaker both carry out the instruction behind the barrier and at the end of the game the barrier can be removed to see if the results are identical.

Children need to be encouraged to say if they did not understand the instruction or not enough information was given.

Social Stories™

Social Stories™ were devised by Carol Gray (see www.thegraycenter.org) and are simple descriptions of expected behaviour. You can illustrate each section of the story with a photograph. Social Stories are widely used to support children on the Autistic Spectrum, but are also useful for children who have SLCN.

Example of Social Story for Connor about sharing

At wet playtime the children can choose toys to play with.

I like the zoo animals.
Some other children like the zoo animals too.

It is good to play next to other children.
Other children are happy if I give them some animals. Giving animals is sharing.

Miss Peters is happy if three or four children put animals in the zoo.

I will try to give animals to other children.
I will try to let other children put animals in the zoo.

Vocabulary Maps

Many children with SLCN have difficulty in storing and retrieving vocabulary. A visual Vocabulary Map like the one shown in Fig. 7 provides a useful mental model for the children, helping them to 'see' the links between words and ideas.

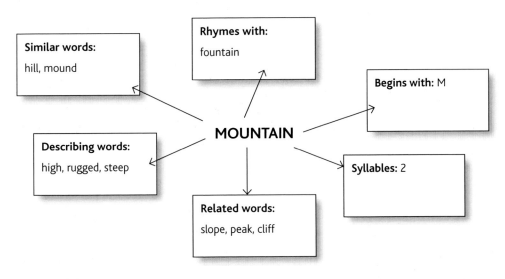

Similar words: hill, mound

Rhymes with: fountain

Begins with: M

Describing words: high, rugged, steep

MOUNTAIN

Syllables: 2

Related words: slope, peak, cliff

Fig. 7: Vocabulary Map.

The Target Ladders

Letters	Understanding the environment	Interaction skills	Verbal language	Non-verbal/visual communication
A	Anticipates familiar situation from something that precedes it (e.g. teacher picking up a lunchbox)	Anticipates interaction event as part of familiar game or rhyme carried out by an adult (e.g. Round and Round the Garden)	Uses voice to get attention	Holds object while looking at it
A	Associates sound with meaning (e.g. looks at teacher when hears shakers)	Takes turns during a very simple interaction with an adult (e.g. taking turns with making noises)	Produces strings of simple syllables (e.g. /bababa/)	Uses an object to achieve a simple aim (e.g. shaking to make noise)
B	Shows change in behaviour when hearing something unexpected (e.g. firebell)	Enjoys slight variations in familiar games and routines (e.g. delaying climax of rhyme)	Consistently responds to a situation to indicate likes/dislikes/wants (e.g. body going rigid shows dislike; rocking shows enjoyment)	Uses gesture to help communicate (e.g. waving)
B	Responds to basic facial expressions in others	Offers objects to adults to initiate interaction	Demonstrates understanding of one or two very familiar words (e.g. 'No', 'Bye' or own name)	Is able to reject an object by pushing it away
C	Understands that an object can be used to indicate something else (e.g. a doll's coat could represent playtime)	Looks towards something indicated by adult	Uses jargon: made-up words that sound like real language	Reaches out for preferred object when offered a choice of two
C	Can be supported using objects of reference to follow a series of events during the day	Enjoys simple 'people-games' and is becoming a more active participant	Understands simple instructions with an accompanying gesture	Points to people or objects to request or show interest

Suggested activities or strategies

Note: The Target Ladder for non-verbal/visual communication is not necessarily useful for children who are acquiring verbal language skills. However, it is an important additional support for children whose verbal language is very delayed or disordered.

Objects of reference

Objects of reference are used with children who do not yet recognise pictures or photos.

- A familiar object is used to represent the next activity, for example, a doll's coat to represent playtime.
- The object is given to the child to look at and feel just before the activity happens.
- A spoken word, and possibly a sign, should be used to accompany the object.

To help the child begin to recognise pictures/photos you can attach a picture/photo to the object (maybe with a bit of string). Show this to the child as they are presented with the object.

People-play

Playing face-to-face interactive games with a child can develop many interaction skills, such as eye contact, waiting, turn-taking and sharing an interest in something. Make sure that your face is at the same level as the child's face. Watch and wait, responding to the things that the child does, then imitate and expand.

You could try the following people-play games.

- Hold some light, semi-transparent fabric between you and the child. Pull it away slowly and show surprise and delight as the child's face is revealed.
- Use rhymes involving the child's body, for example, Round and Round the Garden, This Little Piggy and so on. Use your voice and pauses to build up anticipation.
- Put some favourite objects on the floor in front of you. Reach for one and explore it, then give it to the child to explore. Ask the child to choose a toy and share it with you.

First words

Keep your language short, simple and slow, usually just one or two words at a time. Talk about the things that the child is looking at or interested in. Make your voice interesting. Try to comment, rather than asking lots of questions. The following are examples of good contexts in which to introduce first words.

- Ready, Steady ... Go games, for example, rolling a ball or car, or blowing bubbles.
- Looking at books together. Don't read all the words, just label the main thing in the picture.
- Giving simple, familiar instructions with accompanying actions, for example, '*Wave bye bye*'.

Letters	Understanding the environment	Interaction skills	Verbal language	Non-verbal/visual communication
D	Matches everyday objects to photographs	Shares toy with an adult	Uses symbolic noises (e.g. animal noises, vehicle noises)	With support, is able to hand over a symbol or photo to request continuation of an activity
D	Responds appropriately to a single word, sign or symbol to indicate the next activity	Is becoming aware of other people's feelings (e.g. shows negative response to crying)	Understands 20 single words even without context	Allows hands to be gently manipulated to form a gesture (e.g. song action) or sign
E	With support, uses a Now and Next board to make a transition between events	Demonstrates joint attention by looking between adult and item of interest (e.g. toy)	Copies a few single words	Copies a few signs or gestures
E	Can be supported to use a visual timetable to work through a series of up to four events	Uses person's name/label to initiate interaction (e.g. 'Mummy!')	Uses single words spontaneously to request continuation of an activity (e.g. 'More' or 'Again')	Spontaneously uses single signs or symbols to request continuation of an activity
F	Responds to simple request related to the next activity (e.g. when you say 'It's playtime next' the child gets their coat)	Shows interest in what other people are doing	Makes a choice using a single spoken word (e.g. 'Ball')	Makes a choice using a sign or symbol
G	Independently accesses a visual timetable to work through a series of up to four events	Initiates interaction with other children by making eye contact or handing over an object	Understands at least 50 words	Uses a wide range of signs or symbols to request and comment

Suggested activities or strategies

Joint attention

Joint attention describes the ability to share a social experience with another person. It usually involves the child alternating their gaze between an object and another person.

- Read a book with the child, sharing the pictures. Try to make eye contact.
- Take an object which is interesting to the child. Hold it in front of you, and once the child is interested in it, make your voice interesting and try to get the child to make eye contact with you.
- Put a car on the table in front of you, put your head down so that your eyes are level with the car and then roll it to the child.

Introducing signs and symbols

The use of signs and symbols by a child in order to communicate is often known as Augmentative and Alternative Communication (AAC). See page 29 for more information. Using signs and symbols to help develop the early ability to communicate may be useful but not essential for typically developing children. The use of these visual and tactile cues is of particular value for children with Autistic Spectrum characteristics, specific speech and language difficulties, behavioural difficulties, sensory impairment or a general developmental delay.

Ideas for introducing signs:

- Create a feely bag of a few toys and everyday objects, for example, car, ball, book, cup, teddy. Encourage the child to feel inside the bag and bring out a toy. Say the name of the toy and use the sign. When all the toys are out, say the name and use the sign for each toy and ask the child to find it and put it back in the bag.
- Hide small toys, and see if the child can find them and put them in a box. As the child finds each one say the name and use the sign. Once you have done the activity, ask the child to help you put them away. *'Where's the cow (sign)?'*

Ideas for introducing symbols:

- Play games in which the child has to request continuation, for example, getting a brick to add to a tower, blowing bubbles and so on. Between each turn, pause, giving the child the chance to request continuation of the activity (for example, by looking at you, reaching, making a noise and so on). Encourage the child to hand you – or point to – a symbol which represents that object. As the child hands you the card or points, say the name of the object and let the child have another turn. It is important in the early stages to have only the one card in front of the child that matches the thing they are requesting.
- Once the child has learned how to make a request using a symbol and you feel they are beginning to recognise pictures, you can begin to offer choices. Use two large pictures. Hold one on either side of you, close to the object it represents. Encourage the child to indicate to you which object they want. Over time gradually move the objects so that the child chooses by looking at the symbol alone.

Note: If the Picture Exchange Communication System (PECS) has been introduced for the child you are working with, it is really important that you talk to someone trained in PECS (preferably the person that introduced it to the child) and consult the PECS manual.

Visual timetables

Many children with SLCN have a poor sense of time and they may panic because they are not sure how far through the day they are. In addition to a whole-class visual timetable, prepare an individual, portable one for the child. This individual timetable may give more detail about the current part of the day; for example:

Literacy: carpet time, reading, writing, carpet time. Wash hands. Sandwiches. Playtime.

Letters	Focusing attention	Response to verbal language	Managing distraction	Attention span
A	Concentrates on a preferred object or activity (i.e. attention is voluntary)	Attends to simple language when adult is animated and using gesture	Is not distracted by external stimuli (e.g. someone walking by)	Single-channelled attention for up to 30 seconds
A			Enjoys an activity when adult shares attention	Single-channelled attention for up to 1 minute
B		With support, is able to interrupt attention to listen to adult	Is able to respond to external stimuli (e.g. touch) when concentrating	Single-channelled attention for 1–2 minutes
C	Shifts full attention to adult talk then returns to chosen activity (with support)	Attends more automatically to the language used by adults in one-to-one situation	Switches focus to stimulus with adult's help (e.g. calling name) then returns to activity	Single-channelled attention for 2–5 minutes
C		Waits a short period of time for an adult to give an instruction in one-to-one activities		
D	Shifts attention without support – attends to one stimulus at a time	Alternates full attention between speaker and task (i.e. needs to stop what they are doing to listen to the speaker)	Alternates full attention between speaker and task (i.e. needs to stop what they are doing to listen to the speaker)	Single-channelled attention for 5–10 minutes
D	Controls focus of attention with more ease and purpose	Follows verbal prompt to participate in activity	Can sometimes ignore distractions during small-group activities	
D	Follows visual or auditory prompt to pay attention	Alternates full attention (visual and auditory) between the speaker and the task without prompting	Is able to filter out distractions and keep engaged during small-group activities	Listens to a short story from a picture book for up to 5 minutes in a group

Suggested activities or strategies

Getting the child's attention

Develop classroom routines for drawing children's attention to you before you give them instructions. Try not to use your voice – the children are used to filtering out voices in the classroom. Simple percussion instruments are often easiest.

- Play the instrument.
- Wait until all of the children are looking at you and the class is quiet before you talk.

Any other adults in the room need to model this too.

Visual prompts

- Always wait until you have the child's full attention before giving any instructions.
- Make use of visual timetables – and give personal timetables to the most needy children.
- Keep the timetables accessible to the child in order that they can peel off completed activities.
- Use posters and photographs to demonstrate expected behaviours.

Switching focus of attention

Use activities in which the child has to switch their focus of attention between you and a toy.

- Take turns with objects such as rain sticks.
- Keep hold of the toys. Give the child a choice of two each time.
- Wait for the child to make eye contact before giving them a car to use on a track.
- Place toys in a bag, and wait for eye contact before you offer it to the child.

- Try to get the child to copy you when you play loudly or quietly on a musical instrument.
- Try to get the child to respond to your request to play 'loud', 'quiet' on the musical instrument.
- When you are playing with small world or real world objects, you can try some simple comprehension questions. For example, 'Can you put the tall giraffe in the zebra's cage?' or 'Put the yellow car in the car ferry'.
- When you join the child to extend their imaginative play, use language to describe what you and the child are doing and to suggest other ideas.

Good listening

Teach children behaviours associated with good listening.

- *Eyes* – the children should be looking at the speaker. **Note**: this may not be appropriate for children on the Autistic Spectrum, who find the requirement to make eye contact intimidating.
- *Hands* – hands are not busy doing something else. There may, however, be some children who benefit from a fiddle toy.
- *Brain* – tell the children to switch on their brains. Tell them what you are talking about now.
- *Body* – children should be sitting comfortably or standing in a space.

Take photographs of children showing the appropriate behaviour and display them around the room, particularly near the carpet area.

Letters	Focusing attention	Response to verbal language	Managing distraction	Attention span
E	Refocuses attention spontaneously (i.e. without prompting)	Participates in group actions, songs and rhymes		Joins in chants and repetitive refrains in familiar stories
E	Sits and waits turn in a game or with a piece of equipment	Waits for adult to give next set of instructions during small-group activities		
F	Concentrates on what adult is saying without stopping what they are doing	Continues to focus on task without having to look at speaker		Has brief joint attention
F	Waits for own turn in a game or with a piece of equipment without prompting		Filters out distractions and keeps engaged for brief periods when working in a busy classroom	
G	Knows when it is their turn and re-engages attention	Begins to understand main point of simple teacher talk	Listens and attends as part of a small group for short activities (e.g. 2 minutes each)	Maintains attention on chosen task for 5 minutes

The Target Ladders

Suggested activities or strategies

Sustaining attention in a small group

- Use a visual timetable, with pictures representing each of the planned activities, and ask a different child each time to post the picture when the activity is completed.
- Write some group rules, and use pictures and simple hand actions to reinforce them. That is, the children should do *'Good listening'*, *'Good sitting'*, *'Good sharing'*, and so on.
- Incorporate activities which use music, singing, hand movements and whole body movements to break up the sitting-down activities.
- Try to keep records of the children's progress during the group, under headings such as 'turn-taking', 'attention', 'eye contact', 'understanding of language', 'communication during the group', 'other observations' and so on.

Taking turns

Turn-taking is an important life skill as well as being critical for communication. Children need to learn to maintain interest while other children take turns and to be ready for their own turn.

- Pass a toy around a small group (for example, a rain stick, a click clack track). Get the children to have one go and then pass it on.
- Emphasise the language of turn-taking: *'Mariana had her turn. She found the rabbit. Now it's Danny's turn'.*
- You can ask the children to choose whose turn it should be next. Get them to point, or to say the name of the child. Give them a choice of two: *'Whose turn is it now? Danny's or Ria's?'*

Listening and looking

Looking at the speaker is part of the process of listening, because so much communication is non-verbal. Even children on the Autistic Spectrum should be encouraged to look at your mouth or your ear if they are reluctant to make eye contact.

- Use any toys or instruments. Let the children choose one each. Say *'Ready steady go'*, before letting the children play. Hold up your hand and say *'Stop'*. Let the children have a turn of starting and stopping the 'orchestra'.
- Get a soft ball that the children will find attractive (for example, a glittery ball). Make eye contact with one of the children. Say the child's name, and roll the ball to them. Then encourage the child to think about who to roll the ball to. Encourage them to name that child, or point to that child, to get their attention before rolling the ball to them. Encourage eye contact.
- Make games such as Lotto and Listening Lotto.

Sharing a focus of attention

In order to learn to work together co-operatively, children need to be able to work together, focusing on the same outcome.

- Use a feely bag with one object in it. Pass it round the group and ask each child to say what they think it is and give reasons.
- Work together with construction toys to build a shared structure. In addition to helping each other to add to the structure, discuss what might be done next.
- Build simple Lego® models from plans. Work in twos so that one person is the builder and the other has the plans and the box of pieces. Change roles every 5 minutes.

Following instructions

As well as listening to your voice, it is important for children to be able to listen to their peers.

- Play Follow the Leader. Give one child a drum. Explain that they can make the other children do something when they play the drum. Give the child some things to choose between (for example, *'Everyone jump'*, or *'Everyone clap their hands'*). Model this first for the children.
- Play Simon Says.

Aspect 2: Attention control

Letters	Focusing attention	Response to verbal language	Managing distraction	Attention span
H	Can select stimulus to focus on (e.g. teacher talk or chatter)	Pays attention to teacher talk for 5–10 minutes	Is able to ignore distractions for brief periods while teacher is talking	Completes simple activity while chatting to a friend (i.e. 10–15 minutes' joint attention)
H	Chooses focus of attention in a classroom	Participates in conversations with peers, listening and responding appropriately	Is able to ignore distractions for 5–10 minutes during teacher-chosen activity	Maintains attention on teacher-selected activity (10–15 minutes' joint attention)
I	Starts and completes task with minimal reminders	Listens quietly while others are speaking		
I	Pays attention in class	Concentrates on what an adult is saying without stopping what they are doing	Ignores unwanted, irrelevant information and distractions	
J	Participates willingly in whole-class activities	Makes decision when to listen and focus on teacher	Filters out 'background' talk in class	Sustains engagement for half a day without showing undue tiredness
J	Is able to indicate willingness to get involved by putting hand up	Picks up more detailed information from teacher talk		Completes activity in busy classroom while socialising for 15–30 minutes

Suggested activities or strategies

Using photos as a behaviour prompt

Take photos of the child sitting on the carpet with their hand up. Print a passport-sized photograph and stick it onto a lollipop stick. Ask a TA to sit close to you, in the eyeline of the child, and:

- when the TA catches the child's eye, they can show the child the photo as a reminder of desired behaviour;
- if the child puts their hand up, the TA should reward with a thumbs up;
- when you see the child's hand up, ask the child for their response as soon as possible.

Talking about attention

Help children to understand what you mean by instructions to 'Pay attention' and 'Concentrate'.

- Discuss attention and listening with the whole class, and with individual children. Tell them when they are concentrating well, and give them praise and rewards (for example, stickers).
- Try to get the children to talk about their own areas of difficulty when it comes to paying attention during whole-class teaching (for example, they may know that the classroom is too noisy, or that they cannot remember all of the instructions).
- Provide visual cues and reminders for children with attention difficulties. These could be in the form of pictures of the activities at hand, or words reminding them of the key tasks that they are expected to complete. The children could be encouraged to write or draw these themselves.

Listening skills

Use activities designed to give children practice in understanding and retaining information from talk.

- Play games involving chained instructions such as 'If you have Velcro on your shoes, go and find a jungle animal (toy); if you have laces, go and find a farm animal. Go!'
- There are many published listening skills programmes (for example, Listening Skills 1 and 2 as well as Listen, Think & Do published by LDA). Use these to develop more sustained listening skills.

Picture Mind Maps

In order to help children to understand and focus on information you give, ask a TA to do some pre-teaching (perhaps a day in advance) of key concepts and vocabulary, using picture Mind Maps.

- Provide pictures of some of the concepts you are talking about.
- Model how to link these together in simple Mind Maps. Use coloured ribbon or wool to show links between pictures.
- Give children opportunities to work in pairs to make their own picture Mind Maps while you talk. Provide pictures to enable the children to concentrate on what you are saying.

Wet playtime challenge

Being able to complete a simple task while socialising is intrinsic to being a fully participating member of the class. Use wet playtimes and lunchtime clubs to develop this skill.

- Use 'rainy day' activities such as dot-to-dots, colouring, tangram games, mazes and so on.
- Challenge children to complete a given number of activity sheets during wet playtimes. Encourage children to keep records of the number they achieve each time.

Letters	Imaginative play	Social play	Social interaction	Social confidence
A	Occupies self with exploring toys/objects for a few minutes	Enjoys playing Peek-a-boo and hiding games with adult (e.g. looks for toy under blanket, in a box)	Imitates simple actions (e.g. claps to join in Pat-a-cake-type interaction game)	Does not cry if stranger comes close
A	Mouths, pokes, waves, bangs, drops and passes items from hand to hand	Holds out grasped toy to adult	Responds to speech/action games such as Round and Round the Garden, This Little Piggy	Initiates physical closeness or contact with familiar carer
A	Finds toy that is partially hidden by adult while child is watching	Seeks adult for physical play	Takes turns during very simple interaction with adult (e.g. making noises)	Clings less to known adult in the presence of strangers
B	Looks in correct place for toys that have been moved out of sight	Shows that they want a toy/object (e.g. by pointing or reaching towards it)	Initiates interaction with others (e.g. drops objects for adult to pick up, uses gestures to request simple action games, or offers object to adult)	Shows affection to familiar people (e.g. hugs, pats, kisses them)
B	Can put some items into place (e.g. ring on stacker, one cup inside another)	Enjoys simple 'people games' (e.g. takes turns in give-and-take exchange with adult)	Copies adult, when adult looks at or points to something	Regularly initiates exchanges with familiar adult (e.g. drops pencil and requests its return)
B	Shows functional play skills (e.g. by putting cup/spoon to mouth, brush to hair)	Gives toys to adult on request, and sometimes spontaneously	Repeats actions/sounds if adult laughs at them	Engages in a range of activities when a familiar adult is close by

Suggested activities or strategies

Note: Although most children in mainstream schools have moved beyond these early stages of play and social interaction, it is nonetheless important to understand them. If children have missed out on these early experiences, their social interaction may not develop; in which case the child may need to return to these very simple early experiences. This is often particularly appropriate for children who benefit from Nurture Groups (see www.nurturegroups.org for more information).

Stimulate the senses

Encourage children to explore their environment using all of their senses by providing multi-sensory resources.

- *Listening* – use environmental sounds such as running water, rustling paper, cups rattling, musical instruments that make simple sounds; also play music and sing songs; explore safe items that can be banged/crumpled and so on.
- *Looking* – look at pop-up toys, mobiles, puppets/finger puppets and dangling objects such as coloured shapes or crumpled paper; make the most of human interest (for example, make different facial expressions, use face paints, use colourful scarves/hats/glasses); play simple interaction games such as Peek-a-boo, mirror games, bubble blowing.
- *Smelling* – offer different foods; offer essential oils on a piece of fabric (don't let child mouth them); incorporate food flavourings (such as peppermint, vanilla or almond essence) when making modelling clay.
- *Feeling* – handle different fabrics/soft toys; hard toys; foods; messy play; feel air wafted.
- *Tasting* – offer different foods with different textures and tastes; talk about the taste of daily fruit.

Hiding games

Children and infants need to learn to look for an object when they have dropped it or it has gone briefly out of sight and to recognise that it is still there and it is still the same (this is known as 'object permanence'). Try the following hiding games.

- Play hiding games such as Peek-a-boo, in which you initially partly, and later fully, hide your face/body.
- Once the child is focused on an object, move it partially out of sight (you could partly cover it up with a cloth or put it partly under a box) then bring it out again. Gradually hide more of the item until it is completely hidden.
- Use feely bags – hide an item of interest in a bag and encourage the child to feel inside and bring it out; then hide it again.

Joining in

The key principles for encouraging early social interaction skills are that interaction needs to be with a warm, responsive adult, who shows consistency, and promotes fun and humour. Share activities such as the following.

- Involve children in simple physical play activities such as bouncing on a trampoline holding adult's hands.
- Move in time to simple songs/music/rhymes.
- Give opportunities to watch and begin to imitate simple actions while you sing familiar songs and rhymes.
- *Take turns* – roll a ball to and from each other (or in a small group); pass a bag round and take it in turns to take out, for example, a piece of an inset puzzle; use marble run or roll cars down ramp; pass the parcel; chase games; roll balls/cars; wind-up toys.
- *Eye contact* – hold finger puppets near your face; blow bubbles each time child looks at you (hold wand near your face); play Peek-a-boo using large hats or sunglasses to hide your face and then pull off; wiggle your fingers in front of your face.
- *Facial expressions* – make mouth movements like a fish; pull funny faces; blow raspberries; puff out your cheeks and demonstrate 'popping' them.
- *Use intonation* – make funny voices (falsetto or low voice; up to down; down to up; talk like a duck and so on).

Letters	Imaginative play	Social play	Social interaction	Social confidence
C	Begins to pretend (e.g. pretending to drink or sleep)	Likes to look at simple pictures or a picture book with adult	Demonstrates joint attention by looking between adult and item of interest (e.g. toy)	Engages in a range of activities if a familiar adult is present
C	Imitates and repeats simple activities	Will briefly watch other children playing	Is able to gain adult's attention by indicating or saying name	Will play alongside another child if adult present
D	Uses small world/ role-play resources to represent people to act out everyday events	Engages adult in pretend play (e.g. gives them a cup)	Brings object/book to adult to look at or talk about	Accepts presence of another child when playing without an adult
D	Explores what toys will do (e.g. presses buttons, tries to bend them)	May show parallel play with two or three other children (i.e. come to play alongside them)	Initiates very simple, brief interaction with other children	Plays alone near familiar adult or child
D	Relates two or three items to each other during play (e.g. putting a driver in a truck)	Watches another child play, and may copy their actions	Communicates simply about activity when playing with adult or alongside other children	Comes to play alongside other children
E	Makes symbolic sounds to accompany play	Watches other children play with toys, and will often copy them	Frequently demands attention from main carer	Seeks adult for affection/reassurance
E	Uses one object to represent another (e.g. uses a toy brick as a car)	Occasionally gives toys or food to another child	Listens to other children talking during play	
E	Shows simple sequences in their play (e.g. puts blanket over doll, then puts in buggy)	Shares and takes turns in a short play activity with support	Shows some early interaction with other children	Shows some interaction with other children, with support

Suggested activities or strategies

Learning to pretend

Support children as they develop through different phases of pretend play.

- *Functional play* – using objects for their main purpose, for example, using a hairbrush to mimic brushing their own hair.
- *Self-pretend play* – pretends to do actions without props, such as pretending to sleep.
- *Symbolic play/early pretend play* – relates two or more objects to each other, for example using pots and pans on a toy cooker.
- *True pretend play* – in which one object is used to represent another, for example, using a crayon to represent a car and making symbolic 'Vroom' noises.
- *Sequences of symbolic play* – in which children link sequences of events, for example putting a small world fireman in a fire engine then going to put out a pretend fire.

Symbolic play initially develops with occasional demonstrations of understanding of an object's function (for example, putting a cup to mouth), and increases to short sequences of this. Promote this sort of play by having familiar items present, and if necessary, demonstrating their function yourself and then giving the child the opportunity to imitate this.

Guided play

Give time for play. An adult may need to facilitate the child's early attempts at social interaction during play by participating and modelling.

- Guide the child to play alongside one or two others at the sand tray/in the role-play area/at the work bench and so on.
- If a pair/small group of others are having fun, help the child to come alongside and ensure they have at least one go themselves.
- Prompt the child to sign/gesture/say very short social phrases such as, 'Here y'are', 'My turn', 'Please', 'Funny!' to one of the others. You can demonstrate this yourself first; next time help them gesture/sign by gently moving their arm (if they don't mind this), and saying a word/phrase for them to copy.

- Show and talk about photos/pictures/symbols that represent desired behaviours in the group such as 'Good sitting', 'Time to sit'. Demonstrate if necessary and use the photos/pictures/symbols when children are familiar with them.
- Encourage simple interaction during physical play/running/chasing, for example, by taking it in turns to be the leader and say 'Stop!', 'Go!', 'Go slow!'.

Responding to communication

During play activities and simple interaction groups, use the following principles.

- Observe closely all the child's communicative signals.
- Interpret as carefully as possible all aspects of their communication – being mindful of their likes and interests.
- Respond to their communication (ensuring your response is in line with their developmental level).
- Be prompt in responding to the child (as far as is possible).

Suitable activities to develop communication skills include the following.

- Extend a range of action songs, and create your own versions of these to suit the child's interests, or the theme of the session.
- Activities involving actions, such as copy the leader – bunny hops; crawl; march; waddle; shuffle and so on. Make a large teddy/doll/action figure do actions (have some pictures/photos of actions as prompts) for all these, start by initiating them yourself, and then see if the child will take a turn to make an action for you all to copy.
- Dance to music, or use simple body awareness activities.
- Turn-taking actions – skittles and ball; post shape/picture in box; throw bean bags; take turns to lift flap in picture book/add a brick to tower/put ring on a stick/press buttons on toy/press touch-screen button.

Letters	Imaginative play	Social play	Social interaction	Social confidence
F	Plays dressing up using one or two items (e.g. adult shoes or hats)	Joins in chasing games or physical play with adults and/or other children	Actively seeks interaction with familiar adults, and will initiate interaction with a peer	Will join groups of other children playing
F	Is able to attribute an imagined property to an object or person (e.g. pretending a teddy is hurt/angry)	Is sometimes able to play co-operatively (e.g. build a tower with another child)	Communicates with other children when playing	Is able to join in organised group songs and games
F	Mimes use of imaginary items	Seeks adult involvement in simple sequences of pretend play with dolls, cars, trains and so on	Plays simple turn-taking games (e.g. Snap, Picture Lotto) if guided by adult or older child	Accepts new situations (e.g. a move to different room, different adults) after initial anxiety
G	Talks to self, giving running commentary on own actions in play	Contributes appropriately to simple role-play with at least one other child	Initiates conversation by verbal strategies (e.g. calling a name and forming simple comment/question)	Co-operates in group activities led by adult
G	Enacts specific roles (e.g. being a postman/ police officer)	Co-operates in play with other children at least some of the time (e.g. making a jigsaw puzzle together)	Regularly talks to other children and adults	Is more able to communicate with strangers
G	Uses large boxes/tables as cars/houses (and so on) in imaginative play with other children	Will share and take turns in several play situations (may need encouragement)	Can participate in pretend conversations during play	Separates from parents in familiar setting (e.g. school, club, friend's house)
G	Acts out puppet shows/ TV programmes	Plays more extended board games (e.g. Ludo®) with two or three others including an adult	Is included by others in play as 'good' partner (i.e. waits turn, follows rules, controls frustration on losing)	Enlists adult help when required, with diminishing of clinging or dependence
G	Plays purposefully and imaginatively with small world toys for extended periods	Actively involves other children in play – listens to them and responds with talk	Is able to share, take turns and play by agreed rules	Asserts self appropriately with adults and other children

The Target Ladders

Suggested activities or strategies

Supporting imaginative play

Continue to guide, prompt and scaffold children's symbolic play, giving them frequent opportunities to observe and join in others' playing, and have an adult close by to ensure that opportunities to extend play sequences are not missed.

Some play scenarios can be set up by the teacher.

- Let the children help choose what theme to have in the role-play corner (for example, police station, hospital, vets, post office).
- Have dressing-up clothes available and provide other props the children could use – for example, large cardboard boxes, small chairs, pieces of fabric.

Note: Some children dislike putting additional or unfamiliar clothes on. Encourage them to join in by playing a role/using a prop.

- Use or create puppet theatres and provide puppets for play.

The rules of the game

Children who struggle with social interaction feel more secure and confident when there are clear rules. Often, they like to make the rules – but they will generally accept your rules or the 'official' ones.

- Go over rules for activities and games in advance.
- Have clear visual reinforcement of the group social rules. For example, place 'Good sitting' and 'We take turns' symbols on the wall next to children playing a turn-taking game together.

Social Stories™

Social Stories are short, simple descriptions of desirable/expected behaviour in specific situations. They are particularly useful for regular events, such as assemblies, toileting or sharing. See www.thegraycenter.org for more information. You will probably need to use photos/symbols for the story, unless the child can read. A sample Social Story is given on page 45.

Modelling behaviours

Use role-play, small world people and puppets to recreate simple social scenarios and give children opportunities to see their peers, or adults, responding in appropriate ways.

- Create situations in which the children will need to negotiate over the use of items/toys/props (for example, only have one till or set of scales in the grocery shop if you know both like to be the shopkeeper; or reduce the number of scissors or stamps at the modelling clay table).
- Recreate events which recently caused conflict or distress and discuss what alternative actions could have been taken.
- Set up role-plays about events that are going to happen (such as a class trip or a visiting theatre company) and encourage the children to explore responses.
- Throughout activities, encourage discussion about:
  - desired behaviours;
  - appropriate language;
  - alternatives to undesirable behaviours;
  - how people feel when ....

Letters	Imaginative play	Social play	Social interaction	Social confidence
H	Uses or adapts other children's or adults' ideas in play in imaginative and creative ways	Will conform to rules during small group games (e.g. playing board/card games)	Comments on what others are doing (e.g. progress in a game or task)	Is willing to play or work with less familiar children
H	Takes different roles in group play, improvising props	Has good relationships with other children (e.g. will co-operate, share toys, organise and take turns)	Sustains attention to adult throughout adult's turn, looking briefly at object being referred to	Is confident trying new activities, in a variety of situations
I	Vivid imaginative play – ideas can merge fact and fiction	Is able to regularly play in a small group of other children without adult supervision	Directs others through talk	Is able to contribute briefly to large group
I	Demonstrates detailed role-play, with roles decided in advance, and planned sequences of play	Is able to conform to routines and rules (e.g. recognises when to stop or change an activity, or take turns in a game) and understands fair play	Listens attentively throughout adult talk to group	In a familiar group, has the confidence to initiate talk and introduce ideas
J	Adapts to changing roles in group imaginative play	Is able to play team games with rules (e.g. football)	May guide younger children in their play	Anticipates and tries new experiences without undue worry
K	Engages in highly detailed small world play for long periods (e.g. setting out village scene, or various characters interacting in a palace)	Is able to play co-operative games such as Draughts and Battleships	Discusses a topic with a familiar adult or friend, expressing own point of view and listening to others	Approaches others to ask for help when needed
L	Increasingly distinguishes between fact and fantasy during imaginative play	Is able to play complex indoor and outdoor games (e.g. hopscotch, tag, Blindman's Bluff)	Works well as member of group or team with peers; contributes ideas and listens to others	
M		Begins to show strategy in games such as Ludo® and Draughts	Co-operates in group activities without direct adult guidance	Has confidence to express opinion on ideas discussed

Suggested activities or strategies

Fact and fantasy

Some children feel anxious during free or unstructured playtimes (often because they prefer activities that are predictable and logical). By giving some direction for dramatic play you can help to relieve some of this anxiety.

- Revisit stories – encourage children to act out stories you have read, or dramas you have watched on TV or DVDs. Talk about fact and fantasy. Initially, give prompts and direction: for example, assign face masks, give each child a named character, set out props in certain places.
- Suggest children adapt the story, changing one thing and developing the story from there.
- Check children's understanding of what is real and what is fantasy, especially about things on TV and in films.

Team games

- Reinforce rules of games, visually if necessary.
- Create simpler versions of games, to allow success and maintain interest. You can then gradually build up to a more advanced version. Consider the number of children playing a particular game – fewer children may allow success for a particular pupil.
- A lot of team and playground games involve touch, so consider whether a child may have hypo- or hyper-sensitivity to this. If so, you may need to introduce rules about how touch happens: for example, when playing tag, the players must use a firm but gentle pat on the shoulder only.

Awareness of self and others

Target self-awareness and other-awareness using a variety of social skills/circle time group activities.

- Take it in turns to say what somebody looks like/is good at/likes and so on.
- Take photos of all the children (preferably carrying out different activities) and put them together in different groupings, for example: children who like reading books/playing football; children with dark/fair hair; children who are good at running/singing. Talk about similarities and differences. Let each child summarise about themselves, and/or about another child.

Ensure success

In order to build social confidence, try to avoid asking a child to take part in a game that they do not understand.

- Clarify rules, using visuals if necessary.
- Give the child the props/reminders to enable them to take part.
- Keep the game short enough that the child can remain focused/interested for the complete activity.
- Adapt games to simplify them (for example, make your own version of Pictionary® using easy enough words/concepts, and few enough turns).

Letters	Listening and auditory memory	Understanding vocabulary	Understanding questions and abstract language	Understanding sentence structure
A	Turns to other children in the group as their names are said	Responds to tone of voice (e.g. *'No'*)		Answers yes/no questions with a nod/ shake of head
A	Follows routine phrases (e.g. looks towards table when *'snack'* is talked about)	Gives objects when they are asked for in context (e.g. *'Give me the register'*)		
B	Repeats single words	Can point to familiar nouns (e.g. *car, house*) when looking at a book	Understands *where* questions about the immediate situation (e.g. *'Where's your bookbag?'*)	Understands requests which contain one key word/information-carrying word (e.g. *'Give me the* **brick***'*, *'Where's your* **coat?***'*)
B	Identifies pictures or objects when listening to a tape of familiar sounds	Can do simple actions in context when asked (e.g. *'Walk'*, *'Jump'*, *'Stand up'*, *'Sit down'*)	Understands *what* questions related to the here and now (e.g. *'What are you doing?'*)	
C	Joins in with repeated refrains for familiar stories and rhymes (e.g. *'Run run as fast as you can … '*)	Sorts and selects objects by function (e.g. when shown an apple and a hat and asked to *'Show me what you wear'*)	Can point in response to *'Find another one like this'* when a matching object is shown (e.g. when adult holds up a sock)	Responds to questions offering two choices (e.g. *'Do you want a red pencil or a blue one?'*)
C	Enjoys listening to a short story for 2–5 minutes		Identifies the correct object from a choice (e.g. when asked *'What goes with the fork?'*)	Follows two-key-word instructions with familiar vocabulary (e.g. *'Give the* **book** *to* **Peter***'*)

The Target Ladders

Suggested activities or strategies

Listening games

Before children can make meaning from verbal instructions, they need practice in developing the skill of focusing their attention onto a noise and individual words. Listening games can help.

- Find the animals – hide toy animals. The child is the farmer and has to find the animal when they hear the noise it makes.
- Find a hidden noisy object (for example, use the alarm on a mobile phone).
- Everyday sounds – collect objects/pictures of things a child hears often, such as jangling keys, car engine, dog barking, vacuum cleaner, bell, sneeze and so on. Make the sound or record it on a simple recording device and see if the child can match the sound to the picture.
- Stop'n'Go – Children must wait for you to say or signal 'Go' and 'Stop'. For example, *Jump on the spot and stop when I clap*'.
- Recite familiar songs/rhymes with a puppet – let the puppet 'forget' the words for the children to say instead.

Q and A

Introduce question words: *where* and *what* first.

- *Where* is it? – hide some objects around the room (on the window sill, in the corner) and ask the child 'Where is the ...?'
- *What* is it? – ask the child to tell you what an object is called. Also, show the child an object and ask them to find another one.

What does it do?

In order that children can store and retrieve vocabulary and concepts successfully, they need to learn how ideas are linked. One of the easiest ways of demonstrating this is by focusing on function.

- Tidy up time – tidy toys away when you've finished playing and put each item with other toys or resources with a similar function. For example, all wheeled toys go together; colouring equipment goes together.
- Feely bag – make some bags containing three or four linked objects (for example, animals, transport, fruit). When the child takes an object out of the bag, ask them to name it. When all the objects have been named, talk briefly about how they are linked. *'They are all animals.' 'You can drive them all.' 'We eat fruit'.*
- Pick it up – place four to six objects in front of the child and ask them to pick up the one you ... paint with, play with, eat, throw and so on.
- Puppets – use any puppet and give simple instructions for the child to follow such as *'Go and touch something you sit on'* or *'Find something you can eat'*.
- Develop some simple Mind Maps around topics. Use real objects to begin with. Lay them on a table or on the floor and link them to the main idea using coloured wool or string.

Letters	Listening and auditory memory	Understanding vocabulary	Understanding questions and abstract language	Understanding sentence structure
D	Follows two simple instructions in order (e.g. 'Put the books away then we'll go out')	Can identify early position words (e.g. 'Put the brick **under/on** the table', 'Put the pen **in/on** my desk')	Understands *who* questions about current activity (e.g. 'Who has the frog puppet?', 'Who is jumping?')	Follows sentences with pronouns (e.g. 'Put it on **my** plate', 'Where's **your** coat?')
D	Tries to clap in rhythm to a familiar tune or song	Can choose an object by primary colour or number 1 to 5 (e.g. 'Give me **two** balls', 'Find the **red** pencil')	Understands *when* questions about familiar situations (e.g. 'When do we put on our coats?')	
D	Identifies a target sound or word against noisy background	Understands some describing words for size (e.g. 'Find me the **little/big** car', 'Where's the **fat/thin** man?')	Understands *which* questions (e.g. 'Which one do we dig with?')	Follows instructions with three elements (e.g. 'Put the **book** and the **car** in the **box**', 'Put the **balls** in the **box outside**')
E	Repeats a given sound	Understands some words describing texture (e.g. 'Where's the **soft/hard** ball?', 'Where's the **dry/wet** sponge?')	Understands *where* questions about events outside the here and now (e.g. 'Where did Mog go?' after reading a story)	Understands simple comparative words (e.g. can give you the *bigger* cup or the *smaller* car)
E	Listens, attends and follows short stories and responds by drawing a picture	Can match pairs of pictures/objects from a selection (e.g. toothbrush and toothpaste; bucket and spade; knife and fork)	Can indicate how a character might feel from a selection of 'mood' pictures (e.g. 'How does Mum feel?' when looking at a picture)	Understands the conjunctions *and*, *but* (e.g. 'You can go out **but** wear a hat', 'Put on your hat **and** your coat')
E	Remembers a list of up to four different objects	Understands more advanced positional words (e.g. *behind, in front of*)	Can indicate what might happen next when carrying out a familiar routine such as cooking or getting dressed	Understands regular plurals such as *cars, sweets* and *shoes*

The Target Ladders

Suggested activities or strategies

Remember remember

You can play a wide range of different games and activities to help build and develop auditory memory.

- Drums – play a pattern of beats on a drum and the child can repeat the pattern on their own drum.
- Go and touch – play this outside. Check the children know the names of five or six different things, for example the fence, seat, gate, climbing frame. Say 'Walk to the fence and then run to the seat'.
- Shopping/café game – set up a pretend shop or café. Ask the shopkeeper/waiter for 'the apple and bread' or 'a burger and a cola'.
- Simon Says – the child has to do what you tell them but only when you say, 'Simon Says ...'
- Go! – give an instruction but tell the children to wait until you say, 'Go!' For example, 'Pat your tummy ... go!' Instructions can get harder. 'Touch your nose and turn around ... go!'
- Give sequences of instructions in PE. For example, 'First walk ... then jump'.

Position words

Many children struggle to learn and use position words accurately. Take advantage of regular opportunities where the words have a familiar context.

- Explore position words in PE, for example, by playing music and asking children to sit under something when the music stops.
  Stress the position words throughout your PE lessons.
- Tidying up – use tidying-up time to help to confirm position words: 'Put the whiteboards under the whiteboard pens', 'Hang the aprons up behind the coats'.
- Lining up is an ideal context for introducing language such as at the front, at the back, in front of, behind.

What next?

Understanding sequences is fundamental to reading, writing and number as well as to social development. Literacy sessions, in particular, offer opportunities for discussion.

- Sequencing – put three or four picture cards into the correct sequence, and talk about what is happening in each picture. Later, leave the last picture out and see if the child can tell you what might happen next.
- What next? – show the child pictures of their daily routine. When one activity has finished ask the child to show you the picture of what they are going to do next. If this is too difficult give them a choice of two pictures. 'Are you going to play on the computer or paint?'
- Before you turn the page of a story book, talk about 'What might happen next'.

More than one

Plurals are generally made by altering the last sound in words, and these are the sounds that children frequently find hard to hear and pay attention to. Give them experience of using plurals in games.

- Play barrier games using pairs and single objects. Put up a barrier between you and the child and make sure you both have the same equipment (such as farm animals, felt pens or bricks). Give the child instructions such as 'Put the cows behind the shed' or 'Put the blue bricks in a tower on top of a red brick' while you do the same with your items. Remove the barrier and compare outcomes.
- Plurals – sort pictures of a sock/socks; play Lotto and identify the picture only by hearing the word spoken (for example, car/cars, cup/cups).

Letters	Listening and auditory memory	Understanding vocabulary	Understanding questions and abstract language	Understanding sentence structure
F	Listens attentively	Knows a range of colour names such as purple/pink/light blue	Understands *why* questions (e.g. '*Why does a bird make a nest?*')	Understands *because, to, if, so* and *when* (e.g. '*We will all go out* **when** *Paul comes back*')
F	Gives three related objects in order when they are at a distance (e.g. '*Give me the pencil, the book and the scissors*')	Understands action words used in class (e.g. *cut, draw* and *stick*)	Understands *how* questions requiring problem-solving (e.g. '*How do we copy this picture?*')	Can correctly follow instructions with embedded information (e.g. '*All the boys wearing jumpers sit down*', '*All the children with white trainers go outside*')
F	Gives three unrelated objects in order when they are at a distance (e.g. '*Bring a pencil, a water bottle and a plastic cow*')	Understands instructions with common adverbs (e.g. '*Jump quickly*', '*Walk slowly*')	Begins to enjoy simple jokes	Understands sentences containing reference to future/past events (e.g. '*Tomorrow we'll go to the park*')
G	Can remember four items	Knows names for broad categories (e.g. *animals, food*)	Can understand questions requiring an explanation (e.g. '*What could you do?*')	
G	Can tell you the name of something else in a group when some members of the group are named (e.g. '*Horse, cow and ...*')	Understands abstract verbs (e.g. *choose, guess, pretend*)	Can respond to a statement about why we can't do something (e.g. '*I'm making a model but it keeps falling apart!*')	Understands passive sentences in context (e.g. '*The cat was chased by the dog*')
H	Listens to an explanation to find the answer to a question	Understands homophones (words which sound the same but are spelled differently and mean different things (e.g. *sea/see*)	Can understand questions requiring problem-solving from another person's point of view (e.g. '*What could Peter do if he forgot his coat?*')	Understands the use of negatives (e.g. *can't, won't, hasn't*)
I	Suggests solutions to simple problems or riddles presented orally	Knows which objects belong in a category and which do not		

The Target Ladders

Suggested activities or strategies

What am I?

Simple riddles encourage children to listen, to retain key information and to use that information to identify the answer. These skills are important across the curriculum, as well as socially.

- Select a range of pictures for the child to look at. Describe one of them. For example, '*I have four legs. I have whiskers. I purr. What am I?*'
- Tape a simple picture onto each child's back. Encourage children to work in pairs. One child looks at another child's picture and describes it. The child who is wearing the picture has to work out what it is from the description given.
- Introduce simple riddles, but ensure that the answer can be found in a picture that the children are looking at.

Word families

Many children with SLCN struggle to store, organise and retrieve words effectively. Categorising activities provides them with a model they can use to help with these difficulties.

- Sort it! – sort objects into categories and ask the child to tell you the name for each category. Model it if they are not sure. Gradually add more categories to the sorting game, for example, clothes, food, transport, animals.
- Odd one out – using groups of three pictures, ask the children to sort the two pictures that go together and the 'odd one out'. Start with obvious pictures such as a car, a bike and a cat; an apple, an orange and a spade.

Solve it

Help children to develop language and thought patterns which help them to problem-solve. Describe a simple scenario and ask the children to suggest a solution. For example:

- '*Sanjay is out in the rain. His jumper is getting wet. What can he do?*'
- '*Bridget is chasing her rabbit round the garden. What did she forget to do?*'
- '*You need to draw a square. What do you need to get?*'

Can't, won't, hasn't

These negatives are very common in classroom instructions (for example, '*Who hasn't got a pencil?*', '*Who can't see the board?*'). Play 5-minute filler games to explore them, such as:

- Play a version of Simon Says. Try do/don't instructions, such as, '*Simon says … do a star jump/don't do a star jump*' or '*Sit down/don't sit down*' and so on.
- Identify two zones in the class. Say '*Who has got a younger brother?*' and point to one zone; and '*Who hasn't got a younger brother?*' and point to the other zone. Children move to the correct zone.

Letters	Listening and auditory memory	Understanding vocabulary	Understanding questions and abstract language	Understanding sentence structure
J	Correctly follows peer's instructions in a simple barrier task	Can identify a group within a category (e.g. knows that *melons*, *apples* and *grapes* are fruit and that *potatoes*, *peas* and *cabbages* are vegetables)	Understands and solves riddles	
K	Follows classroom instructions to complete a three-step task appropriately	Understands more abstract descriptive words (e.g. *early*, *late*, *solid*, *liquid*)		
L	Identifies the 'main ideas' in 5 minutes of teacher talk	Understands verbs used in curriculum (e.g. *compare*, *estimate*, *arrange*)	Recognises the emotions and motives of other people	
M	Is able to use strategies to help remember instructions (e.g. visualising, repetition)		Understands idioms (e.g. '*I've got butterflies in my tummy*')	Understands irregular plurals and irregular past tense

Suggested activities or strategies

Guided listening

It is important that children become more independent in remembering and understanding what is said in the classroom. Therefore, begin to teach self-help and clarification strategies such as the following.

- Mind Maps – using colour and branches and pictures helps children to categorise and link words. This makes it easier to store and recall words.
- Action plans – use lists with symbols/pictures to organise a task.
- In maths, ask the child to show you how they arrived at an answer rather than just telling you the answer. Encourage the use of tactile resources for reinforcement.
- Visual checklist – these can be used to help remember instructions. For example:
  - say the instruction aloud;
  - check that you said it correctly;
  - say it again but this time in your head;
  - try and picture what you will do;
  - keep saying it to yourself quietly or in your head.
- Teach the children a 'script' for them to use when they don't understand:
  - ask speaker to repeat: *'Can you say that again?'* … *'Could you say that again more slowly?'*
  - ask for more information. For example, *'I don't know what I have to do'*… *'What does … mean?'*
- Put up a 'Good listening' poster to make explicit the required skills.

Pre-teaching

- Before the lesson, give the children the key words to listen out for – either written or in the form of symbols or pictures. Focus particularly on technical vocabulary and abstract language.
- Help them learn core vocabulary using Vocabulary Maps (see p. 45). Use the same format as Mind Mapping to show other words with similar meanings and related or describing words (for example, for *mountain* you could have *hill, slope, peak, rock, jagged*).

- Give opportunities to explore and experience concepts and vocabulary, particularly in science (for example, *attract, repel*).

Idioms

There are many commercial activities available to support children in learning idioms. These include matching cards and worksheets as well as picture dictionaries. Ensure that you explore any idioms you encounter in your reading together, and check that children properly understand those you use in the classroom (for example, 'Hold your horses', 'Pull your socks up', 'Pull your finger out').

Playing with tenses

Link to oral work to improve writing, with children working in mixed ability groups.

- Let children work in groups of three. Give each child a sign saying 'past', 'present' or 'future'.
  - Ask 'past' to say a sentence in 'their' tense. 'Present' and 'future' should repeat the sentence in their tenses.
  - Let 'present' and 'future' say their own sentences for the other children to 'transform' by changing the tense.
- Challenge children to:
  - find sentences which don't transform well into other tenses;
  - explore what happens when you use the verb *'to be'* as a helper verb (for example, *'I was walking'* rather than *'I walked'*). How does it change when tenses change?
- How many different ways can they find of working with each tense?

Letters	Vocabulary	Sentences	Narrative	Talking together in group activities
A	Names familiar people (e.g. Mummy, Daddy, Grandma as well as teacher and TA)	Uses short sentences with noun, verb and object to refer to current activity (e.g. '*I push car*')	Carries out familiar routines with adult (e.g. putting books away, getting coat for going home)	Knows names of others in the group
A	Names familiar body parts (e.g. *mouth*, *nose*, *eye*, *arm*, *leg*)	'Asks' questions by intonation (e.g. '*You go home?*')	Predicts the next word or sound in a familiar story/poem	Makes a choice in the group by nodding or shaking head
B	Names familiar items of clothing	Uses personal pronoun 'I'	Uses a short phrase in response to questions about familiar books	Gains attention by using someone's name
B	Names familiar household objects		Participates in pretend play sequence without an adult (e.g. pretending to make a drink)	Focuses on what others are doing/saying
C	Comments on size (*big/little*) colour (*red/blue*) or position (*under/on*)	Uses four- to five-word phrases (e.g. '*I push big car there*')	Knows basic daily routine of the school day	
C	Comments on size, (*big/little*), texture (*hard/soft*) or quantity (*all/some*)	Uses *a/the/some* before nouns	Comments on what is happening during repetitive play sequences	Comments on what others are doing

Suggested activities or strategies

Naming

When children are at the labelling stage of language development, emphasise the words you want them to learn. Say those words a little louder, clearer and more slowly than other words in your utterances. For example, '*Go and get your **coats**, then **line up** for playtime*'.

Support children in naming objects in the following ways:

- Talk about what you are doing in simple sentences and leave spaces for children to respond. '*It's break time, so we need to put on our ...*' '*Time for lunch, let's get our ...*'
- Give children clues by offering 'forced alternatives'. '*Is it a house or a car?*', '*Look we've found a book – is it Nicky's or Sarah's?*'
- Have large colourful picture books around in which objects are shown in context. When you look at the books, try to make comments and not ask questions. For example, '*That's a big car. I've got a blue ...*' Children will usually fill the space and then give extra information about what is familiar to them.

Using abstract words

Words for size and texture are harder for children to learn as they can change according to the situation. A toy car may be big when compared to another toy car, but is small when compared to a real car.

- Concentrate on one concept word at a time – for example, *big*. Contrast big and little objects by sorting. Name the objects as you sort. '*Look at these cars. This one is big and this is not big. So we'll put this car with the ...*'
- Use PE activities to encourage the use of 'position' words. '*Look at Fred – he's **in** the tunnel. Where's Fred? He's ...*'

Modelling and expanding

Encourage the use of complete sentences by modelling correct sentences and expanding the child's talk.

- Have three large cubes (for example, *Move Cubes* by LDA). In the pockets of the first cube, stick pictures of various people/animals (nouns). In the second cube, stick line drawings of various actions (verbs), and in the third cube stick a selection of objects or places (these must fit with the nouns and verbs, for example *house/shops/car/beach*). The child rolls each cube to make a silly sentence, for example, '*The **lion** is **running** to the **shop***'. The child may only say '*Lion run shop*' but you can expand it for them.
- Encourage the use of the pronoun 'I' during circle time activities, when other children can model the expected response before you ask the child with SLCN. Simple questions requiring an '*I am*' or '*I can*' response are best. For example, '*How old are you?*', '*How high can you jump?*' If the child says '*Me jump*' model the correct answer carefully with, '*You say ... I can jump this high*'.
- Make reading books with photographs of the child and captions: '*I can ... run/jump*'.

Sequencing language

Use the language of sequencing when you talk about what you are doing. '*First we ... and then we ... and then what happens ... and last ...*'. For example, when tidying up say, '*We put the cars in the box and then we ...*' and allow the child to complete the sentence.

Use the same ideas for dressing up, playing in the role-play corner, making a shop, café or garage, or using puppets.

Aspect 5: Expressive language

Letters	Vocabulary	Sentences	Narrative	Talking together in group activities
D	Names 20 animals (e.g. farm animals, zoo animals)	Uses simple question forms (e.g. 'What you do?', 'Where you go?')	Talks about what they are doing in pretend play sequence	
D	Uses less familiar action words (e.g. '**cross** legs', '**line** up')		Uses *first/next/last* to talk about what is happening	Tells others what to do (e.g. 'You put hat on')
D	Names objects outside the house (e.g. familiar shops and places)	Uses three-element commands (e.g. 'Throw red ball', 'Push big car')	Retells a familiar short story with picture clues	Asks simple questions about an activity to find out more using *what/ who/where*
E	Uses some adverbs (e.g. *quickly*, *quietly*, *slowly*)	Can use regular plurals (e.g. *houses, cars*)	Tells you the next step in a familiar play sequence	Asks *why*, *when* and *how* questions
E	Tells you to place an object *behind/in front of/ next to* something (e.g. 'Put it **next to** my coat')	Uses pronouns *he/she/it* accurately with correct verb (e.g. 'He is reading')	Gives two to three instructions for a familiar activity (e.g. making a sandwich)	
E	Comments on ideas related to quantity such as *empty/full* (e.g. 'My water bottle is empty')	Uses *they* accurately (e.g. 'They are painting')	Tells you the next step in a familiar routine	

The Target Ladders

Suggested activities or strategies

Beginning pronouns

The first pronouns to be learned are generally
I, you, we but many children confuse *he, she, it,
they, them*. Support children with activities
like these:

- Have two large pictures, one of a boy and one
of a girl, together with action pictures in a
bag. Place your boy and girl pictures on the
floor. Let each child choose an action picture
from the bag and then place the action
picture on either the boy or the girl picture.
Before they do this, they need to tell you that
'*He is ...[jumping]*' or '*She is ... [throwing the ball]*'.
Praise children when they use the correct
form.
- Practise three-element sentences using
pictures. Model and expand children's
utterances to include statements like '*She is
throwing the ball*', '*He is walking the dog*'.

Writing frame

- Create a writing frame for the children to use
when writing sentences.

Who	What	And the rest

- under *who* children can write either a
pronoun (e.g. *she*), a name (*Priya*) or a noun
phrase (*the girls*);
- under *what* the child should write a verb
phrase (*is reading, are jumping*);
- under *and the rest* the child should finish
the sentence (for example, *a book, in the
garden*).

What/where/who/when/why

Try to play the following games in small groups
with an adult to model the questions.

- Each child takes it in turn to take a picture
from a bag. They hide the picture under a
template with a shape cut out – so only part of
the picture shows. The child asks the group,
'*What is it?*'
- Let each child take a picture from a secret bag
and tell the group one thing about the picture
– for example, '*It's blue*' or '*You can sit on it*'.
Then the child asks the group, '*What is it?*'
- Choose a picture in a book which shows
familiar scenes. Let one child look at the
picture and ask, '*Where's the ... (banana)?*' The
other children have to look at the picture and
find it quickly.
- Each child takes it in turns to hide a toy
around the room. They return to the group to
ask, '*Where's the teddy bear?*' Encourage the use
of prepositions in the spoken replies.

During these activities develop some cue
cards for each question word to help children
remember the meaning of each – you could
write *where* with a building symbol and question
mark, write *who* on a face, and so on.

Puppet play

Give children the experience of reversing their
normal role of receiving instructions by asking
them to give instructions to a puppet.

- Pretend a puppet has forgotten how to do
some familiar activity or made a mistake
– for example, putting its hat on its hands.
Encourage the child to tell the puppet what to
do. Remember not to rush the child. You may
need to cue by saying, '*First you ...*' Repeat what
the child has said using *first, next, last* and so
on to give a good model.
- Include prepositions in the instructions: '*First
put your bookbag in your tray, then put your water
bottle next to the jug of water*'.

Letters	Vocabulary	Sentences	Narrative	Talking together in group activities
F	Tells you colours including less familiar colours (e.g. black/white/yellow)	Uses third person singular (e.g. 'He wants the ball')	Retells recent past event about self giving one or two facts (e.g. 'I went park', 'I played Dad')	Asks for help if confused, using taught script (e.g 'I need help please')
F		Uses *and* and *'cos* to link sentences	Retells recent past event about someone else (e.g. 'Where's the boy gone?', 'Yesterday went nanny')	Offers a simple solution (e.g. 'Put coat on now')
F	Talks about *one more* (e.g. 'One more chance?')	Produces sentences with four key words (e.g. 'I/go/home/now')	Retells a familiar story with up to four picture cues	Conveys feelings about shared activity (e.g. 'That funny')
G	Tells you if something will happen *today/after/soon* (e.g. 'Soon it be my birthday', 'After three sleeps')	Uses *my, you're, his, hers*	Says what next in a familiar story with no picture clue (e.g. 'Goldilocks wake up')	Joins in role-play in a structured activity
G	Uses comparisons *more/less, heavier/lighter* (e.g. 'That box is heavier')	Uses contracted negatives (e.g. 'He isn't running')		Gives reasons (e.g. ''Cos it isn't ready')
G	Can tell you what is the same/different about two or three objects (e.g. 'That car is red and that lorry is red but the fire-engine is blue')	Uses some comparatives/superlatives (e.g. *bigger, fastest*)	Asks a question about a familiar story (e.g. 'Is Mum happy now?')	Shares the main points of a lesson/activity with group
H	Names items from one category (e.g. 'Apples, oranges and bananas are fruit')	Uses *theirs*	Can say what is next (e.g. 'Now it's playtime')	Expresses a view (e.g. 'I like apples but not carrots')
H		Uses *can't/won't*	Describes an object/person/animal in a familiar story	Extends an idea (e.g. 'Then we painted a picture. Can we make models now?')

The Target Ladders

Suggested activities or strategies

Sorting and grouping

Encourage children to offer reasons for their decisions during activities which teach them to link words and ideas.

- Sorting games – use different coloured hoops and then sort pictures or objects into groups as you name them. For example 'all the things we eat' in one hoop versus 'all the things we wear' in another hoop. Name the categories together as you do this.
- Make a simple Mind Map using real objects and coloured ribbon for the branches. For example, you could make a holiday Mind Map with branches for 'what we do', 'what we wear', 'where we go', 'what we play with'. Then take a photo to save the image for the children.

Describing words

Adverbs are often more abstract than adjectives, but just as important.

- Use a photo timeline to help children talk about *today/after/soon*. Take pictures of what they have done/will be doing and place them sequentially in a line on a board or table. Point to today/now and talk about that. Then slide your finger forwards or backwards to another event and ask, '*Is this before or after today/now?*'
- Use 'Spot the difference' pictures.
- Create two surprise bags. Take an object from each and name one thing that is the same and one that is different for the objects. For example, '*The cat and the chair are the same because they have four legs. They are different because you can't sit on a cat.*'
- 'In the manner of' – choose an adverb, for example, *quickly,* and then ask each child to think of an action, for example, *hopping*. The group then all 'hop quickly'. Get each child to say what they are doing. Prompt with a forced alternative if needed. '*Are you walking slowly or hopping quickly?*'

Hard to hear

Word endings (such as: negatives – *isn't*; contractions – *it's*; plurals – *trees*) are critical in English but are often difficult for children to hear and use.

- Is it yours? – ask each child in the group to contribute an object to a box. Take one object out of the box and say to a child '*(Lynn), is this yours?*' Model the expected response, either '*Yes, it's mine*' or '*No, it isn't mine. I think it's (Joe)'s*'. The child then passes it to the person they named asking the same question you asked – '*Joe, is this yours?*' – in order to elicit one of the two expected responses.
- Sorting games – sort clothes or possessions, modelling correct use of the contracted form of *is*. For example, '*That's my book*', '*That's your pencil*'.

Words like *and, but, 'cos* also cause problems for many children because we say them quickly and they do not sound important to young children. Try activities such as this:

- Linking sentences – have two bags, one with photographs of familiar people and one with a variety of objects. Each child takes one photo and one object from the bags and then makes a sentence mentioning both, for example, '**Sarah**'s got a **plaster** 'cos she fell'.

Using photos or pictures

Take photos of the child(ren) participating in an activity (such as cooking) or find pictures that tell a familiar story, and:

- ask the child(ren) to sequence the photos/pictures;
- having rehearsed it, ask the child(ren) to tell you what happened, using sequencing words where possible;
- cover all the photos/pictures except one and ask the child(ren) to tell you what happened next.

Encourage questions from the rest of the group, by using cue cards (each card showing one question word: *who, what, when, why, how*). Turn the cards over as each question-type is asked.

Letters	Vocabulary	Sentences	Narrative	Talking together in group activities
I	Names items from two linked categories (e.g. food and drink)	Uses common contractions (e.g. *'Billy's sad'*)	Can retell a story based on a familiar plot	Can comment on a story/poem (e.g. *'It's funny'*, *'I like it'*)
I	Can give two or three facts about an object	Uses possessive 's' (e.g. *'Ella's coat'*)	Can provide an alternative ending to a story	Can ask a question to obtain specific information (e.g. *'Why is the bell loud?'*)
I	Says which category an item comes from	Uses other conjunctions *because/when/but/if/so* to make complex sentences		Gives a reason when classifying or comparing objects or activities (e.g. *'It's like that one'*)
J	Says what you do with an object	Uses future tense/past tense	Adds more detail or information than picture shows	Talks about cause and effect
K	Can provide information about a word (e.g. *'It's a long word'*)	Uses tag questions (e.g. *'I can come, can't I?'*)	Can talk about *why* it happened in a story	Remembers/discusses the key points from an activity
K	Can complete and understand familiar idioms	Refers beyond the here and now with time markers such as *after lunch* and *before play*	Gives a sequence of ideas to answer a *what if ...* question	Retells in chronological order some more complex events (e.g. maths or science activities)
L	Appreciates that some words have more than one meaning	Gives irregular plurals (e.g. *children*) and irregular past tense (e.g. *thought*)	Makes the link between two pictures (e.g. an empty sweet bag and a sick-looking child)	Knows where to start/finish when giving information
L	Suggests synonyms for common words	Connects sentences with *however* and *actually*	Creates an original story	Adapts what is said to the needs of the listener (e.g. giving more information when required)

The Target Ladders

Suggested activities or strategies

Visual support

Use as much visual support as you can. Many children with SLCN have difficulty in storing and retrieving vocabulary. By helping them to 'see' links between words and ideas, the visual Vocabulary Map (see p. 45) provides a useful mental model for the children.

- Make Vocabulary Maps for concept words and unfamiliar words and allow children to keep these by them during the lesson. Encourage children to make their own based on your model.
  - Write the word in the centre of the sheet of paper (for example, *horse*).
  - In a box to one side write synonyms for that word (for example, *stallion, mare, pony*).
  - In a box below write words that are linked to the word (*saddle, stirrup, racing, riding*).
  - In a box to the other side write descriptive words (*fast, huge, cute, favourite*).
- Multiple meanings – write a word in one box. Draw arrows from this central box to other boxes. Each of the other boxes explains and illustrates one meaning of the word. For example, *light* = not heavy and not dark. *Trunk* = an old-fashioned suitcase, an elephant's nose, an American car boot.

Tenses

Model appropriate language to discuss events in different tenses. Draw children's attention to word endings ('I play**ed**'), to grammatical structures ('He **was** playing, I **will** play') and to vocabulary items (for example, irregular past tenses such as *caught*).

- Use small world figures and props or finger puppets to retell a familiar story in the past tense. Tell the story yourself first, using the puppets, then ask the child to retell the story using the puppets.

Barrier games

Play more complex versions of the simple barrier game, such as 'Make a pizza' or 'Draw a face'. Use vocabulary such as *smaller/larger, above/below, at the right, towards the side*.

Telling a story

- Use puppets or props in *Storysacks* (LDA) to act out alternative endings to familiar or make-believe scenarios.
- Encourage the children to ask each other more complex questions where they need to think about the answer.
- Make cue cards – these are credit-card-sized cards each showing a 'Wh ...' word: *who, what, when, which, how* together with a visual reminder about what the word means. When children tell a story, they should turn over each card when they have given a relevant piece of information.
- Generate stories together, using props such as miniature dolls, masks, furniture, vehicles that children can select or pick at random from a bag.

Talking games

Understanding what information a listener needs to know is a tricky skill. Games can give children the chance to hear the amount of information that others provide.

- 'Pass the Question' around a circle. Ask each child in turn the same question. *'What's your favourite TV programme?' 'Who's your best friend?' 'What makes you happy?' 'What makes you sad?'* Make sure that you don't ask the child with expressive language difficulties first, because they need to hear model answers spoken by other children before they have to answer.
- One child pretends to be a character from a story – the others ask questions or pretend to interview the character.
- Find some unusual pictures and encourage the children to talk about *why/where/when* it might all be happening.

Letters	Social understanding	Pragmatic understanding	Pragmatic use of language	Non-verbal pragmatics
A	Anticipates, follows and joins in familiar activities (using words or actions)	Understands simple *what* and *where* questions (e.g. '*What's that?*')	Tries to tell about something that's just happened by vocalising, gesturing and using some words	Combines pointing, hand pulling and vocalisation to bring adult's attention to something
A	Will 'dance' and 'sing' to music		Begins to enquire/ demand attention by asking simple questions (e.g. '*What this?*')	Is able to create a question by using rising intonation, signs or gesture (e.g. '*Hot?*')
B	Has learned some simple social rules (e.g. gives cup or bowl to adult when finished; helps when dressing or undressing)	Listens to a simple story from a picture book	Calls to familiar adult	Is able to maintain same topic as adult 50 per cent of the time
B	Shows an interest in pictures (e.g. may look at simple picture book by themselves)	Shows understanding of talk about people or events not present (e.g. '*Mummy's at work*')	With adult, will talk about pictures and comment on the here and now	Varies pitch/tone of voice appropriately (e.g. when talking to a toy)
C	Wants to be like other children (e.g. laughs when they do without understanding joke)	Shows understanding of requests for clarification by repeating original form of the utterance	Gives simple explanations (e.g. '*The cat knocked it over*')	Repairs utterances by deleting, or substituting an element of the utterance (for clarity)
C	Responds to reasoning and may understand need to 'wait'	Shows some understanding that phrases such as '*In a minute*' mean the need to wait	Uses social words spontaneously, without prompting (e.g. '*Hello*', '*Bye-bye*', '*Please*', '*Ta*' '*Thank you*')	Uses changes in volume, intonation and facial expression to make requests polite
C	Makes relevant comments on activity	Follows conversation with adults and responds appropriately with actions and/or talk for a few turns	Asks (very short) *who, what, where* questions to obtain information	Expresses feelings by gestures (as well as words)
C	Accepts simple rules (e.g. the need to sit still when drinking, stop running when told)	Shows understanding of simple stories	Is able to create a very simple narrative. With help, can talk about things seen and done, and things that are going to happen	Is able to maintain same topic 65 per cent of the time

The Target Ladders

Suggested activities or strategies

Circle time activities

Reinforce social integration and understanding of simple rules using circle time games and activities. Try to ensure that each activity has a clear beginning, middle and end.

- Have simple discussions, for example, about likes and dislikes – using props and/or pictures.
- How many? – the group leader asks questions of each member of the group in turn (for example, '*How many people have glasses/are wearing skirts?*') to increase observation/ awareness of others.
- Who am I talking about? – the group leader gives descriptions (for example, '*This person is wearing trousers*', '*They have blue trainers on*') until somebody guesses who they are talking about.
- Act out simple roles for others to copy – for example, how to comfort someone/help them get their things.
- Try reversing roles – for example, a child takes the role of leading a very familiar group activity instead of the adult.

Puppets and props

Use puppets and props as part of role-play linked to familiar stories:

- give the child opportunities for selecting the puppets or props needed to act out the story;
- allow the child to use verbal and non-verbal communication as they participate;
- ask simple questions to elicit responses;
- encourage the child to ask simple questions.

Allow additional opportunities for the child to explore the story independently, perhaps using stick puppets, felt characters and so on.

Eye contact

- In one-to-one situations, wait for the child to look at you before you do something that you know the child likes – for example, blow bubbles.
- Use face paints/scarves/movements near your face to encourage the child to look at your face.

- Play 'copy cat' games in pairs – one child watches the other's actions and copies them.
- What's different? Children in a small group look at an adult's face and say, for example, '*One eye closed*', '*Mouth open*'.

Note: When working with children who have Autistic Spectrum characteristics, be careful about demanding that they look at you in all situations to show that they are listening; some children find it easier to listen when they are not watching someone's face, since to do so can create an overload of sensory information, or a feeling of anxiety.

Vary your voice

The way you talk is often more important than your words. Try varying your voice and talking to the child about how and why you did so.

- Volume awareness – demonstrate different volumes, using a visual reference (for example, a picture of a jet plane for 'loud', car for 'medium' and bicycle for 'quiet'). Then play activities in which the child has to point to a picture to indicate the volume of what they hear, for example, on a CD/TV, or the adult's voice. Act out stories in which some characters have loud voices and others quiet.
- Tone of voice – talk about stories in which different tones of voice are used, for example, Goldilocks. The girl has a 'happy' tone (later 'scared' when found by bears), bears have 'cross' or 'upset' tone, and so on. Use visual representations of different facial expressions, to ensure children link the emotions to the tone of voice.
- Pitch – use visual representations (for example, bird flying high and worms in the earth below) to explore pitch. Hold the pictures in your hand while you model the response when you ask the child to '*Squeak like a mouse*', '*Growl like a bear*' and so on. '*Say "hello" like a mouse*'; '*Say "hello" like a bear*'. Identify the pitch made by musical instruments, for example, chime bars, piano, glockenspiel.

Letters	Social understanding	Pragmatic understanding	Pragmatic use of language	Non-verbal pragmatics
D	Responds quickly to verbal directions or reasoning (e.g. 'If you tidy up quickly, we can have a story')	Shows understanding of discussion of recent events by commenting or responding to questions	Tells others what to do (e.g. 'Don't do that', 'Give it to me')	Approaches adults and children and makes contact appropriately, (e.g. smiles or uses other non-verbal greeting)
D	Accepts discipline, showing an understanding of what's right and wrong	Shows understanding of stories told to small group. Can relate to own experience	Uses language to talk about past and future events and to give information	Identifies adult mood from tone of voice (e.g. 'That's all we need!')
D	Shows some concern for others (e.g. soothes crying child, reports if someone is hurt)	Understands talk about future events (e.g. 'We'll go shopping after dinner')	Retells simple stories	Uses facial expression and intonation to enhance meanings
D	Is aware of socially acceptable behaviour according to situation (e.g. sits quietly in assembly)	Holds brief conversations with adults (minimum of four exchanges)	Is able to initiate conversation by verbal strategies (e.g. 'Teacher, can I go out now?')	Maintains same topic 75 per cent of the time
E	Shows understanding of a range of games with rules (e.g. What's the Time, Mr Wolf?)	Shows understanding of questions from others regarding experiences, events and stories by response given	Is able to contribute simple sequences of information in a small group	
E	Is able to sequence two to four pictures or photos and talk through the story	Shows understanding of story told to large group	Uses clearer referents (e.g. 'I saw the big dog' instead of 'I saw it/that' when listener doesn't know what's referred to)	Changes level of politeness according to the listener and the context
E	Relays a message given orally (e.g. from one adult in the room to another)	Is able to listen to a verbal description of things and name them correctly	Is able to use language flexibly (e.g. tells fibs, denies actions)	When a conversational turn has failed, is able to wait for a pause and take their turn again
E	Conforms to classroom routines and rules (e.g. recognises when to stop or change an activity)	Recognises if others have not understood; responds appropriately to questions or requests for more information	Talks about feelings of characters in stories (e.g. whether they are cross, happy, scared) and can relate them to their own feelings	Begins to control volume when speaking in class

Suggested activities or strategies

Catch them being good

Use 'marbles in a jar' to encourage the child to conform to classroom expectations:

- focus on particular aspects of the child's behaviour, for example, playtimes, unstructured times in the classroom, class teaching situations, independent working;
- establish the desired behaviours;
- explain that you are looking for evidence of the desired behaviours and you are going to try to 'catch them being good'.

Every time you see the child doing any of the desired behaviours, put a marble (or a toy brick, pasta shape, cube or other suitable item) into a container. Each time you give out a marble, tell the child what they have done well. Initially, give out a lot of marbles at any indication of the behaviour. Gradually, make it harder for the child to win a marble.

Before you begin, agree a reward – preferably a class reward so that others help the child to achieve – for example, 5 minutes' extra playtime; an afternoon of Lego®; an opportunity to play computer games.

Barrier games

Barrier games give excellent opportunities for children to practise understanding what the listener needs to know and responding to requests for more information.

- Give both players a busy picture and counters. Ask one child to give the other instructions to put counters on specific locations in the picture (on a dog, on a building, on a child).
- Tell the second child to ask questions to clarify the instructions (for example, 'Do you mean ...?', 'Which ...?')

At the end, both children compare their pictures to check they are the same. Children can then swap roles.

Volume control

Make a 'volume awareness scale' for the classroom. Write labels for your scale: for example, *playground voice, classroom voice, carpet voice, working voice, silence.*

- Take photographs to illustrate how children behave when they are using each voice (for example, on the carpet with hands up, sitting working at a table, chatting to a friend while making something together) and stick them on the scale.
- Use a counter or an arrow and move it up and down the scale to illustrate your expectations.

Responding to stories

In addition to listening to stories and answering your questions, encourage the children to work in pairs to ask and answer their own questions about the text. Give them a word each time to begin their questions.

- *What* did Goldilocks see in the house?
- *Who* lived in the house?
- *How* did the bears feel when they came home?
- *Where* was Goldilocks when the bears came home?
- *Why* did Goldilocks eat the porridge?
- *How* did Goldilocks break the chair?

Letters	Social understanding	Pragmatic understanding	Pragmatic use of language	Non-verbal pragmatics
F	Begins to choose most appropriate timing for attempts to join in other people's conversations	Requests clarification when they have not understood	Conveys simple meanings of words and expresses a range of emotions	Indicates by facial expression (or questions) if they have not understood
F	Understands that outcomes are not always consistent	Shows some understanding of language used to negotiate or bargain	States some beliefs and opinions	Maintains other person's topic 80 per cent of the time
F	Responds to reasoning from familiar adult about effects of behaviour on self and others	Enjoys sustained conversation (10+ turns) with other children or adults	Uses language appropriate for a range of classroom purposes (e.g. recounts an incident, explains rules and so on)	Produces an average of five utterances per topic
F	Understands what is right/wrong and why	Is aware of some less literal meanings (e.g. 'Hold on', 'For ages', 'The middle of the night')	Teases or jokes in conversation with other children	
G	Shows developing sense of humour (e.g. can see the funny side of minor things that go wrong)	Shows some understanding of similarities and differences in the meaning of words by simply explaining		Uses non-verbal response to demonstrate that they are listening
G	Shows some social restraint (e.g. does not overreact if things don't go well)	Is able to distinguish between fact and fantasy	Is able to take communicative turns in a range of situations and groups	
H	Is able to more comprehensively take the perspective of another person into account	Fully comprehends extended conversation between two other people on a familiar topic	Is able to include some relevant detail in explanations	Indicates breakdown in conversation by looking puzzled and repeating words with questioning intonation
H	Shows some social resilience (e.g. is able to cope with losing a game, or with some criticism/ rejection)	Is aware of some metaphoric usages of language (e.g. 'Caught in the middle', 'Head in the clouds')	Is able to use language to bargain and negotiate	Is able to distinguish between contradictory words and tone of voice (e.g. 'That's nice!' in an angry tone)

Suggested activities or strategies

Playing with language

- Jokes – children can often be helped to understand jokes and riddles if they are taught the structure/formulae of them. A good way to target this is by helping the child (or group) to produce a book of jokes/riddles (most copied, but some invented). Puns tend to be the easiest type of jokes to understand, as they rely on the multiple meanings of a word, or similar-sounding words. It's often possible to use visual illustrations to show the different meanings of the words involved.
- Idioms and metaphors –clearly explain the meaning of idioms and metaphors as they arise in conversation/lessons/stories. For example, *'He's feeling under the weather'* means *'He's feeling a bit poorly today'*. Be very aware of the language that you use to children (such as *'Kick the bucket'*, *'Raining cats and dogs'*). It is easy to forget that everyday phrases such as *'I'm up to here with it'* or *'At the end of the day ...'* may also be taken literally and thereby misunderstood.

Note: Children who take verbal idioms literally may also take visual images literally. For example, they may assume that if somebody in a picture has their eyelids down (even if they are sitting/standing) then the person is asleep (when they may be looking down/blinking).

Problem-solving and negotiation

Set up 'real life' scenarios for children to explore. Base the scenarios on events that are relevant to your class. For example:

- Sam wants to join in a game but Tom doesn't want him to because he knows that Sam will try to take over the game;
- Lucy hasn't been invited to a party but lots of other girls have;
- Kieran is stuck on his work but doesn't want to tell the teacher because he thinks he'll get told off.

Monitor children's use of language for problem-solving and negotiation. You may want to participate to model appropriate language structures and to teach 'set piece' scripts, for example, *'Please can I play?'*, *'I see what you mean'*, *'I understand what you're saying'*, *'Can you explain that a bit more?'*.

Games to explore tone of voice

- Practise mixed messages and discuss examples, such as saying *'I'm happy'* in a very sad tone, or *'I like you'* in an angry voice. Discuss the different meanings conveyed and what this might mean (try to isolate particular examples from real life or TV dramas, such as a teacher being sarcastic about behaviour in the dining room).
- Use appropriate picture books to promote discussion involving appropriate word emphasis (for example, *Would you rather ...* by John Burningham encourages statements such as, *'I'd rather eat mashed worms'/'I hate snail squash!'*).
- Play a Guess what? game. A group member takes a picture/card out of a bag and says/reads what's on it (for example, *'My cat's poorly'*, *'I've won a trophy'*, *'My bike broke'*). Each of the other group members must give a verbal response (for example, *'How awful!'*, *'You lucky thing!'*) and this is followed by a discussion.

Letters	Social understanding	Pragmatic understanding	Pragmatic use of language	Non-verbal pragmatics
I	Feels true remorse for harm they may have caused	Indicates lack of understanding by asking about unfamiliar word	Makes reference to rules of language and communication (e.g. 'You mustn't swear at school', 'You didn't say that nicely')	Conversational repairs improve in maturity
I	Is aware of fashions and trends in dress, hairstyles, music and gadgets	Understands that some words can mean more than one thing	Is able to explain that the same word may have different meanings in different contexts (e.g. *nail*)	Requests clarifications when necessary
J	Shows good understanding of cause-and-effect relationships	Shows awareness of listeners' needs (e.g. in attempts to set the scene)	Shows flexibility in use of indirect requests and other indirect forms (e.g. hints)	Shows awareness of how intonation cues affect meaning
J	Shows good awareness of own level of comprehension by asking for clarification when necessary	Topics of conversation extend into abstract ideas	Uses language to plan, predict, reason, hypothesize and explain	Understands social conventions relating to body language (including facial expression, gesture, posture, distance and eye contact)
J	Makes more subtle distinctions between communicative functions (e.g. promise and prediction)	Responds appropriately to idiomatic, figurative and non-literal language	Sequences and organises events in stories in more complex narratives	Gives clarification in conversation
J	Can assess a communication and comment on where it has gone wrong	Is aware of the politeness of various forms of request	Develops use of non-literal language, (e.g. idiom, simile, metaphor)	Is consistently able to distinguish between contradictory words and tone of voice
K	Is able to see other people's points of view	Shows good understanding of a range of threats and promises	Uses cohesive devices in spoken language	Referents are nearly always made clear
K	Takes account of listener's thoughts and feelings, as well as their individual history and personality	Adapts style of speech to match the listener and the context	Uses sarcasm and irony with peers	Recognises sarcasm and irony and responds appropriately

Suggested activities or strategies

Managing difficult situations

Divide children into groups of three: have a speaker, a listener and an interrupter. The speaker relays some information simply about something that happened to them recently and how they felt about it, and:

- the listener responds and asks questions to elicit further information;
- the interrupter talks constantly about a topic of their own choosing which does not relate to what the speaker is talking about.

Allow all of the children to talk about their experience of the activity and how it made them feel. Discuss how they coped with their feelings. Extend the discussion to comparable contexts experienced by the children in school. How do they manage their feelings?

Exploring language use

Ask children what they think changes in their language when they are talking to their friends, younger children, adults they know well and adults who they do not yet know. Depending on the age and maturity of the children, help them to consider aspects such as:

- tone, volume and pitch of voice;
- amount of interruption;
- choice of vocabulary;
- types of sentences;
- use of slang and informal language;
- body language;
- variation in tone of voice.

Working with the children, create a grid showing these aspects of language.

Try to set up contexts in which children have the opportunity to interact with people from the different groups. Ask one child to engage with the speaker while another makes comments on the grid. Allow children to talk about what they found out.

Developing cohesion

Cohesion is about making links between what you're saying now and what you previously said. Point out that pronouns, repetition of words and phrases and use of articles (*a*, *the*) all contribute to text cohesion, both written and oral. Use books that you are reading together, as well as your teaching of writing, to introduce the idea of cohesion.

Encourage all children in the class to tell each other – and indeed you – when they are finding it hard to follow what a speaker has said because cohesion was not secure.

Sarcasm

Check the child's understanding of what sarcasm means. Talk about contexts in which it is appropriate and how the speaker conveys their intention to be sarcastic.

- Make a simple game.
  - Give each child three strips of paper. Ask all of the children to write or draw one thing they like or hate on each strip. Fold the strips of paper and put them in a hat.
  - You decide a sentence starter, such as '*I really like ...*', '*I don't like ...*' or '*I am scared of ...*'. Let one of the children pick a strip of paper. They should use your sentence starter and make a sentence about the thing on the paper. (For example, '*I really like maggots*'.) Ask the child to use their voice and their body language to emphasise whether they are being serious or sarcastic.
  - Ask all of the other children to decide what each speaker was trying to convey.

Letters	Developing phonological awareness	
	with support	independently
A	Uses tokens to represent the number of words in a short phrase (e.g. adult says '*black cat*' and child shows two tokens)	
A	Counts the number of beats in a short drum rhythm (up to three)	
B	Claps out the number of syllables in one- and two-syllable words in unison with teacher (e.g. [dog]; [ba-by]; [app-le]; [house])	Uses tokens to represent the number of words in a short phrase
B	Claps out the number of syllables in one- and two-syllable words following teacher's model	Counts the number of beats in a short drum rhythm
C	Claps out the number of syllables in one-, two- and three-syllable words in unison with teacher (e.g. [hop]; [flow-er]; [e-le-phant]; [pup-py]; [aer-o-plane]; [cake])	Claps out the number of syllables in one- and two-syllable words while teacher says words
C	Claps out the number of syllables in one-, two- and three-syllable words following teacher's model	Claps out the number of syllables in one- and two-syllable words independently
D	Claps out the number of syllables in one-, two-, three- and four-syllable words in unison with teacher (e.g. [he-li-cop-ter]; [tree]; [di-no-saur]; [mon-key])	Claps out the number of syllables in one-, two- and three-syllable words while teacher says words
D		Claps out the number of syllables in one-, two- and three-syllable words independently

The Target Ladders

Suggested activities or strategies

Syllable Snap

- Put out pictures of words that have two syllables (for example, *carrot*, *apple*, *tiger*, *monster*).
  - Say the first syllable of one of the words (*ap*). Can the child say the second (*-ple*)?
  - If they can finish the word, give them the card.
  - When they have won all of the cards, ask them to say the first syllable for you to finish the word.

Spot the rhythm

- Sing two familiar songs or rhymes with the children.
- Say to the children that you are going to clap the rhythm of the first line of one of the songs.
  - Clap the rhythm.
  - Can the children tell you which song you clapped?
  - Ask them to clap the rhythm while you sing the words again.

Syllable sort

- Find pictures of words that have one, two, three or four syllables.
  - Ask the child to say the words and clap the syllables.
  - Ask the child to find all the words that have: two syllables (such as *tiger*); three syllables (such as *crocodile*); four syllables (such as *alligator*).
  - Can the child sort the words again independently?

Find it

- Clap a number of syllables.
  - Ask children to move around the classroom and stand beside an object that has that number of syllables.
  - Once children are confident with the items in the classroom, clap the syllables and ask them to draw a response on a whiteboard or to tell a talk-partner what they're thinking about.

Name that rhythm

- Clap children's names. Use both given name and family name in order to create a more distinctive rhythm for each child.
- Initially, clap together with the child and you say the syllables in the child's name.
- Once the child is able to join in confidently, invite them to echo you so that you clap and say their name first, then they copy.
- When children are all able to clap the rhythm of their name, help them to learn to clap and say the rhythms of common classroom words and phrases such as:
  - Good afternoon Mrs Wilson;
  - sandwiches;
  - school dinners.

Letters	Developing phonological awareness	
	with teacher/in a group	**independently**
E	Judges whether two words rhyme (e.g. Does *toe* rhyme with *cake*?)	Selects two rhyming pictures from a given set
E	Joins in with generating strings of rhyming words	Is able to produce rhyming strings (real or nonsensical) (e.g. *hen, pen, ten, fen, sen, ren, when*)
E	Joins in with rhyming games (e.g. Rhyming Snap, Football Phonics)	Is able to generate a rhyming word (real or nonsensical) (e.g. *dog* and *frog*; *man* and *zan*)
E	Judges whether two words rhyme when they are phonemically similar (e.g. Does *kiss* rhyme with *kick*? Does *house* rhyme with *mouse*?)	Selects two rhyming pictures from a given set which includes words that are nearly rhymes (e.g. Does *coat* rhyme with *boat*, *cart*, or *road*?)
F	In a group, makes sets of objects and pictures which begin with the same sound	Is able to select objects/pictures beginning with the same sound
F	Joins in games and activities to identify initial sounds	Generates a word that begins with a specified sound (e.g. '*Tell me something that starts with /d/...*')
F	Plays Alliterative Snap in a group	Generates words with the same initial sound (e.g. '*Tell me something that starts with the same sound as ...*')
F	Listens to an adult saying the sounds in a CVC word and selects a relevant picture. (e.g. adult says '*b-u-s*' and child selects picture of bus)	Imitates an adult saying the sounds in a CVC word and blends them before selecting picture (e.g. adult says '*b-u-s*'; child says '*b-u-s, bus*' and selects a picture of a bus)
F	Uses 'phonic fingers' to represent the number of sounds in a CVC word (e.g. adult says '*fish*' and child holds up three fingers)	Segments phonetically simple words into individual sounds (e.g. *on* into *o-n*; *cart* into *c-ar-t*)

90   *The Target Ladders*

Suggested activities or strategies

Note: Not only is rhyme an important skill to learn for developing auditory discrimination and phonological awareness, but it is an accepted fact that it is closely linked to developing literacy skills: children who struggle with rhyme tend also to struggle to read and write. It is worth persevering if children struggle with rhyme because it will impact on their literacy attainment.

Playing with rhyme

- Read nursery rhymes and nonsense rhymes aloud to the child.
- When the rhymes are familiar, re-read them, but pause before the second word in each rhyming pair and allow the child to complete the line.
- Give the child access to poems and rhymes on CDs, DVDs or the internet.

Rhyming names

When you're choosing children to work in groups, use rhyming nonsense words to identify children (for example, '*Stand up if your name rhymes with* **Felleanor**; **Sallum**').

Strings of rhymes

Teach children the strategy of using the alphabet to make strings of rhyming words and non-words. For the purposes of this activity, don't distinguish between real and invented words. Give the children a simple word to start them off, such as *man*, and ask them to make rhymes: *ban, can, dan, fan, gan* and so on.

Rhyming games

- Play commercially available games such as *Rhyme Lotto* and *What's the Rhyme? Sorting Houses* (both from LDA).
- Make games such as Rhyming Snap, or a rhyming memory game, by downloading images from the internet and making them into playing cards.

Worksheets

- Download or make simple worksheets.
- Although rhymes need to be spoken aloud, children can work independently or with a partner to:
  - cut out pictures and stick them down in rhyming pairs, or draw lines to show rhyming pairs;
  - find the odd one out and cross out the word in a row of pictures that doesn't rhyme;
  - cut out and make sets of words that rhyme.

Introducing analogy

- If children are already reading and writing simple words while they still grapple with rhyme, use CVC (consonant–vowel–consonant) words as your rhyming sets and write the words under the pictures.
- Help children to find what-is-the-same and what-is-different about two words that rhyme.
- Help children to use this understanding as a strategy for spelling.

Using ICT

The internet is full of interactive rhyming games to play with a whole class or small group using the interactive whiteboard, or individually. In addition to resources from UK companies such as the BBC, you'll find that there are many American sites. It's fine to use these, but play the games yourself first just to check that the rhymes and words 'work' for your children.

Letters	Auditory discrimination	Speech sound production/articulation		
		end sounds	**beginning sounds**	**middle sounds**
G	Identifies the difference between two non-speech sounds (e.g. shaker and tambourine)			
G	Identifies the difference between three or more non-speech sounds (e.g. drum, shaker and tambourine)			
H	Correctly identifies most sounds in a discrimination task (e.g. Picture Sound Lotto game)			
I	Hears the difference between two speech sounds (by correctly selecting their symbol)	Imitates the target sound in isolation (e.g. /f/ /s/ /k/)		
J	Hears the difference between two completely different speech sounds in VC or CV nonsense words, (e.g. /oop/ versus /ook/ or /poy/ versus /koy/)	Imitates the target sound in a nonsense word by blending vowel and consonant sounds (e.g. /eef/ /oos/ /irk/)		
J	Hears the difference between two speech sounds in real words (e.g. *ape* versus *ache* or *pea* versus *key*)	Imitates the target sound at the end of a VC or CVC real word (e.g. *if*; *roof*; *ice*; *mouse*; *ache*; *park*)	Imitates the target sound at the beginning of a nonsense word by blending consonant and vowel (e.g. /fee/ /soo/ /kir/)	
J	Hears the difference between two speech sounds in CVC real words (e.g. *lip* versus *lick* or *pat* versus *cat*)	Uses the target sound independently at the end of a VC or CVC real word	Imitates the target sound in a CV or CVC real word (e.g. *four*; *farm*; *sea*; *soap*; *car*; *king*)	Imitates the target sound in a VCV nonsense word by blending vowel-consonant-vowel (e.g. /eefee/ /oosoo/ /irkir/)

The Target Ladders

Suggested activities or strategies

Notes: In this Target Ladder only, you should complete all the targets in a column before you begin to address targets in the next column.

Work on one sound at a time in end, then beginning, then middle position. Only when that sound is secure should you switch focus to another one.

The sounds /f/ /s/ and /k/ have been used as examples in these targets for no other reason than these are sounds that many children have difficulty using. If the child you are working with has difficulty with other speech sounds, such as /sh/ or /t/, substitute those sounds.

Minimal pairs

Minimal pairs are a useful concept in working with speech sounds. A minimal pair is a pair of words in English that vary by only one sound. It can be the first (for example, *sea*, *pea*) the last (*sea*, *say*) or the middle (*seep*, *soap*). When you are working with a child on developing speech sound discrimination, it is better to concentrate on varying the consonant sounds because that is what children struggle with.

- Say pairs of CV (consonant–vowel) words and non-words, for example *see*, *pea*; *car*, *tar*; /noo/, /koo/. Can the child tell you whether they are the same or different?
- Say pairs of VC (vowel–consonant) words and non-words, for example, *ache*, *ate*; *ark*, *arm*; /oop/, /oot/. Can the child tell you whether they are the same or different?
- Many sets of minimal pair pictures are available from sites such as www.blacksheeppress.co.uk.

Imitating and producing speech sounds

- Ask the child to copy a target sound in isolation based on an adult model (the adult always demonstrates first). Give the child a reward as a positive reinforcement of their attempts and/or correct production of the specific sound.
- Ask the child to copy the target sound in a nonsense word based on an adult model (the adult always demonstrates first). For example, /eef/ or /orf/ (end sounds); /fee/ or /foo/ (beginning sounds); /eefee/ or /oofoo/ (middle sounds). Aim to have no break between the vowels and the target sound and make sure that the child doesn't use any other sounds in between.

Bear in mind that nonsense words are easier to imitate and produce than real words because they have no meaning and therefore 'bypass' any habitual speech sound production error.

Try the following ideas for choosing the vowel sound to blend together with the target consonant sound:

- go fishing for vowel sounds using magnets tied to string to catch fish with paperclips on their noses – each fish should have a vowel sound written on it;
- use a feely bag of vowel sounds;
- hide vowel sounds around the room for child to find and then blend;
- hide vowel sounds in the sand tray;
- have the child 'post' the vowel sounds in a toy post box when they have blended the sounds;
- find monster pictures and give each monster its own vowel sound (look at the position of its mouth and try to make it appropriate: for example, a smile is /ee/, a roar is /ar/, pursed lips is /oo/);
- have 'stepping stones' with vowels and the target sound written on for the child to copy as they step on each 'stone' to cross the room.

Letters	Auditory discrimination	Speech sound production/articulation		
		end sounds	**beginning sounds**	**middle sounds**
K	Hears the difference between two speech sounds in more complex words (e.g. *lollipop* versus *lipstick* or *penguin* versus *kitchen*)	Imitates, and then uses, the target sound independently at the end of a more complex word (e.g. *giraffe*, *police*, *music*)	Uses the target sound independently at the beginning of a CV or CVC real word	Imitates the target sound in the middle of a real word (e.g. *laughing*, *café*, *juicy*, *messy*, *walking*, *bucket*)
K	Hears the difference between two similar speech sounds in VC or CV nonsense words (e.g. /oot/ versus /ood/ or /sar/ versus /zar/)	Imitates, and then uses, the target sound independently at the end of a word in a short phrase (e.g. 'a green *leaf*', '*new dress*', '*pick* it up')	Imitates, and then uses, the target sound independently at the beginning of a more complex word (e.g. *feather*, *sandwich*, *candle*)	Uses the target sound independently in the middle of a real word
L	Hears the difference between two phonemically related speech sounds in VC or CV real words (e.g. *at* versus *add* or *Sue* versus *zoo*)	Imitates, and then uses, the target sound independently at the end of a word in a longer phrase or sentence (e.g. '*I'll huff and I'll puff* ...', '*The horse ate the grass* ...', '*We played in the park*')	Imitates, and then uses, the target sound independently at the beginning of a word in a short phrase (e.g. '*four boys*', '*yellow sun*', '*carry a bag*')	Imitates, and then uses, the target sound independently in the middle of a more complex word (e.g. *saxophone*, *sausages*, *sticker*)
L	Hears the difference between two phonemically related speech sounds in CVC real words (e.g. *write* versus *ride* or *sip* versus *zip*)	Uses the target sound in connected speech	Imitates, and then uses, the target sound independently at the beginning of a word in a longer phrase or sentence (e.g. '*The farmer is in the field*', '*On Saturday I saw my Nan*', '*Can you see the cow?*')	Imitates, and then uses, the target sound independently in the middle of a word in a short phrase (e.g. '*He's coughing*', '*It's icy*', '*In my pocket*')
L			Uses the target sound in connected speech	Imitates, and then uses, the target sound independently in the middle of a word in a longer phrase or sentence (e.g. '*A puffin is a bird*', '*My laces are undone*', '*He's cooking chicken*')
L				Uses the target sound in connected speech

Suggested activities or strategies

Speech sound production

The following activities can be adapted for the chosen target sound at the end, beginning and middle of words. The sound /f/ has been used in the examples below.

- *Single words* The child copies and then uses the target sound in real words from an adult model (the adult always demonstrates first). This could be potentially a very boring exercise for the child so make it as much fun as you can!
  - Put a selection of objects or pictures (with the target sound at the end/beginning or in the middle) in a feely bag for the child to choose; then model the word and have the child imitate it ('*You found a leaf! fish! coffee!*') and then have the child try it on their own. Use a reward system that shows the child how well they are doing and motivates them to 'do more'.
  - Choose objects or pictures to hide around the room and be found by the child.
  - Find pictures to 'hang' on a 'washing line' when named.
  - Use pictures of words with the target sounds at the end to make resources such as Lotto, Pairs, Snap! You can look for pictures on the internet or buy them from sources such as www.blacksheeppress.co.uk.
  - Select objects for use in Kim's Game. '*What's disappeared? Yes it's the scarf! fork! starfish!*')

- *Short phrases or sentences* The child copies and uses the target sound in a short phrase or in a longer phrase or sentence when talking about pictures/objects in a game. For example, '*I've got a ... scarf*', '*A knife is sharp*', '*I've got a ... fan*', '*The phone is ringing*', '*I've got the ... elephant*', '*Toffee is really sticky*'. Use books with target sounds and encourage the child to retell the story. For example, '*The wolf said "I'll huff and I'll puff ..."*' and '*The Giant said "Fee, fi, fo, fum ..."*'.
- *Generalising into everyday speech* At this stage, the child should be starting to generalise the target sound in words so that even in their everyday conversation, you notice that they are using their 'new' sound.

Note: Be aware that, as a general rule, children may not develop blends until approximately 5 years of age. They may be able to say words such as *sea* and *key* but may not be able to blend consonants to produce words such as *ski*.

Blends/consonant clusters such as /sp-/, /fl-/, /cr-/, /str-/ have not been targeted here. To work on blends, follow the same pattern as the targets for single sounds:

- final place in nonsense words: /ee**sk**/;
- initial place in nonsense words: /**sk**oo/;
- final place in real words: de**sk**;
- initial place in real words: ***sk**eleton*;
- in short phrases: '*school **sk**irt*';
- in longer phrases: '*My brother has a **sk**ateboard*'.

Links to other *Target Ladders* titles

Other books in the Differentiating for Inclusion series may well include targets which will be appropriate for some dyslexic learners. For example:

Target Ladders: Autistic Spectrum

Louise Nelson

Includes additional targets for:

- Social interaction
- Getting attention
- Non-verbal interaction

Target Ladders: Behavioural, Emotional and Social Difficulties

Rachel Foulger, Sue Smallwood and Marion Aust

Includes additional targets for:

- Social interaction with peers and adults
- Controlling emotions
- Coping in the classroom

Target Ladders: Dyslexia

Kate Ruttle

Includes additional targets for:

- Phonological awareness
- Auditory perception
- Phonics and spelling

Other useful resources from LDA

How to Identify and Support Children with Speech and Language Difficulties   Jane Speake

CVC Word Spin

I Hear with my Little Ear   Liz Baldwin

Move Cubes

Phonics Lotto

Pull Your Socks Up!

Rhyme Lotto

Social Sequences - At Home

Social Sequences - At School

Understanding Emotions   Mark and Katy Hill